the Ex *factor*

Relationship Baggage
and How to Deal With It

Emily Dubberley

First published in 2007 by Fusion Press,
a division of Satin Publications Ltd
101 Southwark Street
London SE1 0JF
UK
info@visionpaperbacks.co.uk
www.visionpaperbacks.co.uk
Publisher: Sheena Dewan

© Emily Dubberley 2007

A catalogue record for this book is available from the British Library.

ISBN: 978-1-905745-17-3

2 4 6 8 10 9 7 5 3 1

Cover illustrations by Janice Tividad
Cover and text design by ok?design
Printed and bound in the UK by
Mackays of Chatham Ltd, Chatham, Kent

To everyone who's ever helped me get over an ex, in whatever way

Contents

Acknowledgements

When the idea for this book first came along, I wondered if there would be enough material to fill it. I called some mates for drinks and inspiration. We started talking about exes and by the end of the night, I realised I'd have a hefty editing job to do.

Exes offer a minefield of material to (carefully) plough. Almost every woman has tales about her favourite ex and 'the bastard' (generally the bastard gets more stories); most have bunny-boiling confessions; and too many have had broken hearts. Obviously, I've shamelessly stolen stories from almost everyone I've met (along with hundreds of people who emailed me), albeit after changing names, to help me write this book. I've also relied on friends for cocktails, escapism, flat-pack building (I can't focus if the flat's a mess and the storage situation is getting desperate), massage (yeah, OK, in my dreams), music and general support.

Particular thanks go to Rachel Fountain, who almost managed to keep me sane while I was finishing this book and certainly kept me fed and healthy(ish), and Mil Millington, for providing literal back-up throughout (yet again).

Other stars include: Sarah Allcock, Louisa Allen, Sarah Bee, Immodesty Blaize, Dawn Buckler, Anne Cantelo, Avril Cooper, Scott Dendy, Nicky Falkof, Euan Ferguson, Alyson Fixter, Mat Fraser, Caroline Gold, Sarah Hedley, Peter Jarrette, Sarah Lewis, Linda McCormick, Monmouth, Pintxos People, Vesna Pivcevic, Catherine Quinn, Su Quinn, Mark Sandeman, Greg Stekelman, Tammy Weis, The Wetspots (Cass King and John Woods) Chrissy Wright, everyone on the Bloggers with Book Deals mailing list and the readers of *Scarlet* magazine.

Thanks are also due to all at Vision for helping this book become reality, my agent Chelsey Fox, and my family, in particular Jean Dubberley, Juliet Dubberley, Jason Goss, Heather Kesterton and Becky Goss, for not complaining too much that I spend my life writing about sex and relationships. And of course, to all my exes: without you, this would have been a lot tougher to write.

Introduction

In any relationship, there's one thing you're almost guaranteed to have in common with your partner: exes. Unless you're very young, very innocent or very choosy, it's unlikely your lover is going to be the first you've ever had or vice versa. And while it's easy to say the past is in the past, in reality things can be very different.

You man's ex can be the cause of rows for myriad reasons: because you found a photo of her that's altogether too flattering – or she's naked – and you want to know why your partner's kept it; because she's still in love with your other half and won't stop stalking him; because your man is still recovering from the broken heart she gave him (or he gave himself) and takes it out on you; or because she was with your partner for so long that she's friends with all his mates, who indiscreetly pass comment on how fabulous said ex was. Nowadays, an increasing amount of people stay friends with their ex, so you may even have to deal with them in person. And then there's all the fun that comes if your partner has kids with his ex.

The Ex Factor aims to deal with all these issues and more. What should you do if your man's ex still treats him as her shoulder to cry on or an emergency wallet? How do you avoid crossing the line between suspicious snooping and bunny-boiler behaviour if you suspect something's not quite right? Is it acceptable to ask a partner to get rid of all souvenirs of previous relationships? And is there ever a good reason to ask, 'Am I better than she was?' Find out what the way your partner treats his exes says for the future of your relationship, and learn all the essentials of ex-iquette.

And it's not just your partner's exes that can cause a problem. This book also looks at the dilemmas you may face through your own exes. How do you get over an ex in the first place? What are the signs that you're genuinely ready to move on? How long can you pine for an ex before it becomes unhealthy behaviour? Should you ever have sex with an ex? Can revenge be a good thing or does the fact that you're even considering it mean that you're a psycho? Is trying to stay friends with an ex needy and desperate or healthy and adult? And if you do make the attempt to be friends, how should you handle it when they – or you – get a new relationship?

The Ex Factor also looks at the best ways to tell your partner any details about your exes – and whether that's the right thing to do. Should you admit to how many exes you've had, or blur the figures to make yourself sound 'better'? Is there any benefit in admitting to your man that he's not the biggest or best guy that you've had the fortune to get naked with, even if asked directly? When your relationship's going through problems, is it OK to ask an ex for advice? In these days of floating sexuality, how should you handle it if you find out that you've got an ex in common with your lover? And how do you negotiate the complication of running into an ex in the street when you're with your new partner – particularly if the previous relationship only ended recently?

Relationships are hard enough to negotiate when there are only the two of you to deal with. The last thing you need is an ex lingering around the place physically or psychologically to make things even more complicated. If you've ever dated before, and plan to again, you need this book.

A note about sexuality

Nowadays, sexuality is accepted as being a considerably more fluid thing than it was in the past. Women can be heterosexual, homosexual, bisexual, bi-curious or refuse to label themselves as anything other than 'sexual' with much less stigma than was once the case. This is a wonderful thing. However, it makes it a nightmare to write about sexuality – all those 'he/she' sentences just look ugly. As such, I've assumed that the majority of readers are broadly heterosexual, as they form the bulk of the population. That said, in the main, people are people, so the advice given here will work whether you've got male or female exes (or both). There are situations in which sexuality becomes more pertinent with exes – for example, if you discover that you've copped off with your boyfriend's ex-girlfriend — and I've dealt with those cases on an individual basis. Regardless of your sexuality, I hope you find the book useful. If you're really offended by the amount of 'hes' in the book, feel free to doctor your copy with a biro and turn them into 'shes'.

Chapter 1

The Different Flavours of Exes

Once upon a time, people waited to have sex until their wedding night. They saved their virginity like a magical gift to bestow upon their partner as the ultimate sign of love. While that's all very sweet and romantic, nowadays such behaviour is so far from the norm it seems like a thing of myth. By the time most people reach their mid-20s they're likely to have had a handful of sex partners at the very least. And although casual sex is on the increase, it's more often the case that there has been some semblance of relationship to go with the nooky. So, like it or not, unless you marry your first love, you'll have exes to deal with.

If life was a fairy tale, your exes would vanish in a puff of smoke. Sadly, there's no potion or spell around that will make that happen and it's bad form to hire a hit man to get rid of everyone you've dated. Instead, you have to deal with them in a grown-up and mature way, no matter how boring that may sound.

Some exes are polite enough to make themselves scarce and never darken your door again once a relationship ends. And then there are the majority: the ones who are still in love with you – or hate you and want the world to know what a nightmare you are. The ones you still pine after even though self-loathing shoots through you with every drunken text message. The ones who dump you only to return with declarations of love the second you meet someone new. The ones that you know were a mistake but still can't help thinking of every time you're enjoying a ménage-à-moi. The ones you have to see every day at work. No matter what nightmare scenario you can envisage, there's a potential ex to fill it. After all, love is blind – and it's only when you split up and the rose-tinted glasses fall off that you truly realise how short-sighted you've been.

If you're a perfectly balanced and healthy individual, once you've split up with someone you'll forget all about them and move on with your life. However, perfectly balanced and healthy individuals are a rare breed (if they exist at all). It's more likely that you'll end up cursing an ex's name or crying into your pillow – sometimes both – at least for a while. Every relationship has a narrative and until you've figured out the beginning, middle and end of the story in your own head, it can be tough to move on.

This isn't helped by the fact that there are two people in a relationship, so your version of events may differ from your ex's. Everyone wants to be a good person – or at least 'in the right' – and will mentally tailor their version of events to fit that image, however subconsciously. As a result, you can find yourself in a mental loop, going over the same point again and again, trying to figure out what *really* happened. And just when you finally figure it out, you may find yourself back at square one (or worse) should you actually talk to your ex. It can be all too easy to obsess about how things went wrong, or consider endless alternative ways that you could have behaved, which would have meant things ended differently – or didn't end at all.

Dumping lines decoded

One of the toughest things about first splitting up with someone is figuring out what they really meant when they said all those things in the death-days of the relationship. It's the material of pub conversations everywhere. Indeed, if you put five single women in a room together for anything over an hour, with enough bottles of wine, you can almost guarantee that one of them will get out her mobile phone and ask the others to decode what her ex really meant in that last text. It's the law. To make things easier, here's a quick guide to what men say and what they really mean:

He says: It's not you, it's me.
He means: It is you but I don't want to have to explain that your voice is mildly too squeaky, that I hate your taste in music and the way you tap your fingernails on the dashboard when I'm driving makes me want to commit homicide.

He says: I don't feel ready to settle down.
He means: I don't fancy you/I've met someone else that I fancy/I want to have sex with other people.

He says: I need some space to figure out who I am.
He means: I don't fancy you/I've met someone else that I fancy/I want to have sex with other people.

He says: I love you but I'm not in love with you.
He means: I'm crap at relationships and this is getting too heavy for me to deal with.
or
I don't fancy you/I've met someone else that I fancy/I want to have sex with other people.

He says: I'd like it if we can stay friends.
He means: I'm hoping that we'll still get to have sex but that I can shag other people and not have to do all that complicated boyfriend stuff, such as buy you dinner first.
or
I like you but I don't fancy you, though I still won't rule out the occasional drunken fumble when I'm desperate.
or
I'm scared of you and worried that if I say I never want to see you again, you'll hit me.

He says: I'm moving to another country/going travelling.

He means: … and I want to sleep my way around the world.

or

You're a scary bunny-boiler mentalist and unless I say I'm moving to a different country, I'm scared that you're going to stalk me.

He says: It's just not working.

He means: It's just not working.

Look on the bright side: at least you didn't have to suffer the line that one poor girl did, on the website www.soyouvebeendumped.com: 'You mean more to me than life itself but I'm suicidal so f*&^ off.'

It's only once you've got the narrative resolved that you can put an ex in their rightful place – the past. Although every relationship is different, there are some common themes, and categorising your ex may help you move on.

Identify your exes

First love

It's been said that the first cut is the deepest, and that's almost certainly true. If you're lucky you'll have got your first love over and done with in your teens, thus having an understanding mum to reassure you that you will get over it, no matter how terrible you feel at the time (or annoying siblings to remind you that you were dumped because you smell).

If you're less blessed then you may not fall in love for the first time until you're in your 20s, 30s or even 40s. This is more likely to be problematic. In the case of the former, it's unlikely said ex is going to still be causing you that many problems by the time you hit your 30s. Sure, you'll have fond memories but in the same way that you have fond memories of wearing electric blue mascara/drinking alcopops/waking up without a hangover the morning after/not having to pluck your nipple hair: as something from your youth. Chances are that the relationship ended because you were too young to settle down and needed to get out and experience life some more. That's easy enough to rationalise and all your friends will agree that your analysis is right.

If, on the other hand, you reached your 30s or older before anyone stole your heart, it can be harder to deal with. By that stage, most people think they have some semblance of wisdom (because most of them do). As such, you may think that your judgement is off, and make any potential future partner jump through hoops before they get anywhere near your emotions because you don't want to get hurt again. You might hold everyone up against the unachievable fantasy of your first love. Or you could find yourself playing endless games in an attempt to get one over on your partner, to make up for all the hurt your ex caused: by hurting other men, you're implicitly hurting your ex.

The thing that you need to realise about first love is that nothing will ever feel the same second time round. But there's every chance that it could be even better, as long as you don't let yourself get so fucked up by your first experience that you're no good to anyone, least of all yourself.

The love of your life

In some cases, your first love is also the love of your life: someone you felt was a soulmate. But somewhere along the line, things went wrong. However, if you did fall in love as a teenager, it's pretty likely you'll have repeated the whole experience at a later date (see, your mum was right – there really are plenty more fish in the sea). Nowadays an increasing amount of people seem to meet someone when they're in their 20s, fall head over heels in love – 'properly' this time, not like teenage love, or so you tell yourself – date for a few years, move in together or get married and only then realise that things just aren't working.

Of course, you don't have to have dated someone for a long time to consider them to be the love of your life. Passion is a complex thing, and sometimes a brief fling can result in intense feelings.

When the relationship ends with the love of your life you could find yourself making the same mistakes as people make about their first love. You might even see it as proof that love doesn't really exist because you've met your soulmate and it didn't work out. Obviously this will make you a bundle of laughs. If you want to find a future relationship, you need to get rid of any negative thoughts that have been inspired by old relationships.

The thing to accept about the love of your life is that you're almost certainly idealising them. Sure, they gave great foot massages, laughed at your silliest jokes, smelled great and looked into your eyes and made you melt. But you're probably forgetting that they also hogged the remote control, didn't get on with your friends all that well, put sour milk back in the fridge and trimmed their toenails in bed.

What you need to do is bring things back to reality. Write a list of all their good points and bad points. Chances are, because you split up, the negatives will outweigh the positives. And if you can't think of any negatives because they're the one that dumped you? Well, there's the biggest negative of all. Perfect as you may remember them, they didn't want to be with you. And who wants to spend the rest of their life with someone that doesn't want to be there?

The bastard

Lots of women go through a phase of only dating men who are bad news. Generally speaking, they grow out of it once they realise that being stood up, criticised or cheated on (sometimes all three) just isn't fun. Either that or they simply get better at spotting the guys who are bad news and leave them for someone else to deal with (albeit occasionally with a wistful sigh of 'what if…?')

The Different Flavours of Exes

The bastard can be particularly hard to get over because of the way that he plays with your self-esteem, first offering you affection, passion and interest, then withdrawing it, making you feel like you've done something wrong and need to do something to make it up to him and thus earn back his love. In doing so, you end up trying too hard and then get accused of being 'needy'. Before too long, the relationship's ended and you're sitting around thinking that you're the one who messed things up. You didn't. He's just a knob. However, a run-in with a bastard can taint your view of all men, making you defensive or man-hating. This is hardly likely to put you in a good state to find or maintain another relationship.

If you've got a bastard ex, accept that you'll probably never get a real answer about why you split up. He just went off you because that's his wont: he was too immature (regardless of his real age — it's not just young guys that can be bastards) to be able to cope with a proper relationship. He's incapable of intimacy with anyone, and even if he met a supermodel rocket-scientist millionaire chef nymphomaniac, he'd find something wrong with her. Of course, he won't admit that to anyone, least of all himself, so to mask it he'll invent endless reasons why you weren't good enough for him: you wore the wrong perfume, were bad in bed, didn't have a brain, his friends hated you — the more hurtful and liable to destroy your sense of self-worth, the better. Don't let him get to you. His criticisms are there to hide his own insecurities and make you feel as if everything was your fault, because he's not man enough to admit to his own flaws.

It's also important to remember that most men out there really aren't that bad. OK, there are a few out there that are pond scum but generally, you attract what you think you deserve. So if you're insecure as hell, you'll attract men who are going to treat you badly (hence the 'bastard cycle' where you feel low, date a bastard, he trashes your confidence, you feel lower, you attract someone who's even more of a bastard and you end up assuming that every man in the world is the progeny of Attila the Hun, Casanova without the cute bits and the Marquis de Sade without the fun bits). Work on your confidence; stop assuming the worst and you'll find that all men aren't bastards. Really.

The stalker

Studies have found that up to 30 per cent of women have been stalked, and it's generally by someone they already know. It can be annoying, terrifying or even life-threatening. Even at its lightest level, it can make you feel uncomfortable going about your life in the way you normally would.

If your ex refuses to acknowledge that things are over despite being told, you need to get firm and reiterate your point. Tell him that you don't want to see him or speak to him. Don't suggest that you can be friends as a way to appease him – it will only keep him hoping for something more. If he's doing anything that you find intimidating, keep a diary of his behaviour, noting down times, dates and exactly what he's done or said and don't be scared to report him to the police.

To minimise an ex's opportunities to stalk, don't share any information with him about what you're going to be doing (or put it anywhere public, such as a blog or on Facebook). And don't feel too ashamed to tell people about it: it's your ex's problem, not yours, and sharing what's going on with your friends will give you much-needed support and, quite possibly, could help keep you safe.

The sex god

Sex is a powerful thing, and whichever ex gave you the best sex of your life is liable to evoke a strong memory, both physically and mentally. As a result, they can be hard to get over, particularly if you're highly sexed. You may find your thoughts drifting to the sex god ex when you're getting it on with your new partner (or worse, inadvertently shouting out his name), leading to feelings of guilt. You might also think that you're never going to find sex that good again, and end up repeatedly drifting back to said ex just so that you can get your fix of hot action. But remember, sex isn't enough to base a relationship on. No, not even if he does that thing with his tongue and his little finger that turns you into Niagara Falls' wetter sister.

The first thing you need to do to get over this ex is to stop thinking about the sex, even when you're masturbating; or rather, particularly when you're masturbating. Every time you wank with an image of your ex in mind, you're helping carve the memory deeper into your subconscious; added to which, you're unlikely to remember any awkwardness (even the best sex has occasionally squelchy moments) so you're creating an ever more idealised view of your ex, which is hardly going to help you get over things. It might be difficult to resign such a reliable memory from the wank bank but you have to be tough if you want to move on. Delete any dirty texts or emails you still have from your ex, no matter how horny they make you, and invest in some porn to help replace the pervy images in your head with something new. Either that or go with the old 'get over one man by getting under another' rule, if you're secure enough to handle it, are happy with casual sex, and always use condoms.

Above all, feel grateful that you've experienced a sex god. At least now you know that you can have mind-meltingly great sex. Once you've got that knowledge, you can train future men to be the sex god's equal – and then his better.

The mercy ex

If you're lucky, you'll have managed to get through life without ever suffering the mercy shag. However, what with binge drinking being common and insecurity even more so, you shouldn't be all that surprised if you've ended up having a mercy shag in your past. All it takes is a bit of a battered ego and someone you'd never usually consider suddenly becomes someone you welcome with open arms (and legs).

If your self-esteem is low, it can feel like an emotional comfort-blanket to have someone around that adores you, even if you're not that into them: being adored can boost your self-worth, after all. It's only when you start to dread seeing your mercy shag that you realise you've made a terrible mistake and you've been dating them for the sake of your ego, not because you actually like the person concerned. Ironically, once you realise this, it can send your self-esteem back through the floor because you realise how low you're prepared to sink (and you've let someone you don't actually like that much near your nether regions).

If you're lucky, your mercy shag will have been a one-off, but some people are so caught up with being 'nice girls' or hate the idea of hurting someone's feelings so much that they end up in a mercy relationship that obviously fails, leaving them with a mercy ex.

If you're the one who ended the relationship, it's easy enough to get over it (assuming that your ex doesn't turn into a stalker – see page 14). But if they're the one who ended it you can have a whole heap of fun wallowing in self-loathing. Being dumped by a mercy shag can pulp your ego more effectively than a top-of-the-range juicer. You may find yourself questioning your identity – if someone you didn't consider dateable can dump you, what does that mean for people you *do* consider dateable?

Don't let yourself get into this negative train of thought. Should someone you were dating out of pity split up with you, it just means that they were astute enough to read the signs that you weren't that into them and were getting in there first so that you didn't get to break their heart. Ego has a huge part to play in relationships – particularly when they end – and they were just trying to protect theirs, unfortunately for you at the cost of yours. Remind yourself that you didn't want to be with them, breathe a sigh of relief that you don't have to be the one to dump them and learn from the experience so you never end up having a mercy relationship (or even shag) again.

The invisible ex

Always a tricky one, the invisible ex is someone you pine over even though *you never actually dated them*. In some cases, this is a best friend of the opposite sex who you spent every hour of the day with until they landed a partner. In others, it can be someone you considered a hot prospect and spent hours blathering to, only to discover they only ever saw you as 'a friend'. Or it could be that they're gay.

The thing that makes this kind of ex particularly hard to get over is that you're likely to feel like an idiot for developing feelings for someone who didn't reciprocate, and it's highly unlikely you'll be able to cry on your mates' shoulders about it because you feel too ashamed. You may even have to sustain a non-sexual relationship with the object of your desire while pretending nothing is wrong in order to maintain the friendship.

Assuming that you want to keep this person in your life, the best way to get over them is with a bit of distance. Tell them you're going to be busy for the next fortnight (or however long you think it'll take) so you won't be able to chat to them. Keep in mind, however, that being 'busy' for a couple of months is acceptable; a year isn't. Spend this time going out without them and filling your life with new and exciting things and people (you're allowed a maximum of a couple of evenings crying and navel-gazing – though you'll probably find staring at your navel somewhat dull, and it may be worth finding a cute boy whose navel you can gaze at instead). Once you've your sense of perspective back, resume the friendship, keeping the fact that you will never go out with them at the front of your mind.

If you don't think you'll be able to manage that, the only option is to sever contact entirely. And remember, for future reference, that you don't get to keep people 'in reserve' for relationships. Either have the guts to ask them out or accept that you're just friends. Marriage pacts in which you promise to get together with a friend if neither of you have met 'the one' by age 30/40/50 almost never end up happening. If you haven't dated someone, they're not really an ex. Got it?

The 'all his fault'

Everyone has flaws but few people like to admit it. As such, it's not uncommon for people to pretend that all their weak points are someone else's fault. You're always late? That's because your ex used to make fun of you for being uptight about getting to places on time. You can't commit? That's because your ex broke your heart and made you wary of love. You have a drink problem? That's because your ex got you into a party lifestyle then abandoned you. You get depressed? That's because your ex annihilated your self-esteem and you've never fully recovered. It's not your fault, any of it, it's all down to Mr All His Fault.

Get real. Sure, your ex may have done all those things and more, but you don't have to carry around the baggage he gave you as a badge of honour. You're a big girl now — dare I say it, even a woman — and if things go wrong in your life, it's your responsibility to sort it out. Blaming other people for your problems won't get them solved. Sure, it's a way to keep your ex's memory alive. Indeed, some people even think that unless they mourn for their ex for an extended period of time, and carry around a tonne of flaws as a result of them, the relationship was worthless — but that's hardly a healthy thing.

So dump the baggage. Get rid of it with a controlled explosion. Move on with your life. As long as you keep carrying the baggage, you'll end up taking your ex into every relationship you have and if you're going to have a three-way relationship, there are much more fun ways to do it.

The colleague ex

Although the colleague ex can fall into any of the above categories, they also have the additional complication that you have to see them every day at work. See, *now* you can understand why so many workplaces have a 'no dating' rule.

To avoid complication, it's well worth sitting down and hammering things out with the colleague ex when you first break up so that you can avoid sniping over the photocopier or bursting into tears mid-meeting. Don't even think of flirting with other people at work to make your ex regret what they did. OK, think about it but for Christ's sake don't do it. You'll only make things worse.

The druggy/alcoholic

And then there's the substance abusing ex. If you're lucky, you'll never run into one of these, but nowadays drink and drug culture is so rife that it's more likely that you will. The problem with this type of ex is that they're not living in reality. You may well split up with them only to have them on the phone the next day, in blissful ignorance that you're no longer together. You might have to put up with phone calls from them in the early hours of the morning, proclaiming how much they love you, or even proposing marriage. Or you might hear through the grapevine that they've told everyone they dumped you, even though the opposite is true.

The only healthy way to deal with a druggy or alcoholic ex is to stop taking their calls until they face up to their problem. Anything they say is going to be based on an artificial reality – they're talking through a haze of booze or drugs. They have infinite scope to damage you by telling you lies (a symptom of alcoholism/substance abuse), hurling abuse at you or creating their own warped version of reality, in which they're perfect and you're in the wrong. As such, unless they get onto a treatment programme, you have to set them adrift. It may sound harsh but the last thing you want is to get dragged down by someone who's broken and not prepared to fix themselves. Even if an addicted ex does decide to get treatment, AA recommends that addicts avoid relationships for the first year, so there's no hope of you getting back together with them to form a healthy relationship in the foreseeable future. They need to deal with their problem on their own.

* * *

Of course, these aren't the only categories of exes out there. Every interaction with another person is unique so there are limitless ways to describe past relationships. Here are just a few of the labels that the women questioned for this book used to describe their exes: Mr Just Not Right; the cheat; the loser; the wimp; the wanker; dickface; the unemployed drummers (there were many); the evil ex; the stupid mistake; the insecure freak boy; Mr Floppy Bunny; the mummy's boy; Mr Strange; and the self-hating queer.

Hell hath no fury indeed! And it's not just the occasional ex that ends up getting a negative nickname. Some people seem to have worked their way through a veritable boy-buffet of badness.

Ali's story: Too many wrong men

Christ! Who haven't I had when it comes to lousy men? There was the alcoholic control freak, followed by the immature virgin control freak, followed by the doormat, followed by the drug dealer (who was also a immature commitment-phobe), then back to the doormat who by then had turned into an uncommunicative immature commitment-phobe who liked to pretend I wasn't there yet had developed a strange taste in sexual tricks (I thought he was the love of my life – I was wrong). In between these longer-term relationships were the unobtainable hurt-when-I-was-19-so-I've-never-trusted-a-woman-since freak, the fireman (oh yes!), the rich guy

I didn't fancy, the younger man who blew off a weekend in bed with me for an Ultimate Frisbee tournament, as well as a few reckless snogs and fumbles. Thank God I've finally found someone who isn't an idiot.

Other women decide to save creativity by sticking to just the one name for all their exes.

Cara's story: They blend into one

There's a bit of an in-joke between me and two close mates that all my exes are known as 'Shithead'. One conversation went as follows.
Me: So anyway, Shithead?
Mate: Er, which Shithead do you mean?
Me: You know, SHITHEAD Shithead.

However you describe your exes, to horribly misquote Shakespeare, 'an ex by any other name can still leave a nasty smell.'

Identify his exes

It's not just women that get hung up on their exes. Men can be just as bad – if not worse. So what should you do if your other half has ex issues? Well, if you can be bothered to hang in there rather than dumping him and leaving him to sort his own head out, you need to tailor your actions accordingly.

First love

His eyes go misty when he talks about her. You go on holiday together, he recommends a tea shop you should visit and when you ask how he knows about it, he says, 'I came here once with [insert ex's name here].' Whatever you try to do – socially, emotionally or sexually – she's got in there first.

Unless he's constantly bringing her up, there's only one thing to do: get over yourself. Yes, he's fallen in love before. But so have you, most likely. He's not with her any more. And look on the bright side – she was the one who had to put up with his early grimace-faced pube-spitting attempts at oral sex; she was the one who had to teach him that comedy boxer shorts really aren't a good style choice; she was the one who had to face his mum for the first time and machete through the forest of maternal emotion to make your man remotely relationship-worthy. She did the hard work, you got the benefit. Hell, you should probably send her a bunch of flowers.

But what if he isn't able to finish a sentence without mentioning her name? Well, you need to think seriously about whether that's the kind of relationship you want. There's a strong risk that your man is still emotionally involved with his ex, even if he never sees her. As a result, he may take his unrequited love out on you, belittling you by comparing you negatively to his idealised ex – a woman that no-one could ever match up to. Alternatively, he may throw himself too rapidly into the relationship with you, blowing your mind with romance and declaring love before he really knows you, in the hope of replicating the past and using your existence as a way to drown out his memories of his ex. Sometimes this works but more often, the second a problem arises in your relationship, he'll be off because you don't match up to his ex's imagined perfection. Even if things go well between you, there's a chance that he'll feel uncomfortable once you get seriously emotionally involved with each other because it brings back memories of the last relationship he had, which ended up hurting him.

Then again, there *is* a chance that time will heal him and one day you'll notice that he's gone a week without bringing her up. You're the only one that can judge what stage your man is at and whether you're prepared to put up with the emotional hand-holding required in such a relationship. But unless you're really passionate about a man and think he could be 'the one', it's an awful lot of hard work to put yourself through, for potentially minimal reward.

The love of his life

If it was the first love, see above. If not and he's still talking about her, be careful. Deep down, men are often more romantic than women and they can also take way longer to get over relationships. If he's not over the love of his life you're going to have to put in a lot of hard work to make him yours and you have to question whether it's really worth it. There's also the risk that you'll get him over her, only to watch him vanish into the sunset with someone else because, thanks to you, he's finally ready to have a proper relationship again —

but it can't be with you because you remind him of how damaged he used to be.

If you're totally convinced he's the man for you, don't even try to compete with the love of his life – you'll never measure up because she's so idealised by now she's about as realistic as a unicorn. Be yourself. Show him there's something better – and different – to enjoy. And if he still doesn't stop talking about her? Treat it in the same way as you would if he kept wittering on about his first love. You're the only one that can decide whether you want to spend your life listening to your man talking about another woman.

The bitch

The male equivalent of the bastard, men can have one of two reactions to a bitch of an ex. They either turn into withered-up shells of their former selves, with insecurity oozing out of every pore (sexy) or they swear that they're never going to be treated that badly again and, as such, resist every suggestion you make (even ones such as, 'Do you fancy going to the pub to watch the football while I ply you with free drink, then take you to your favourite restaurant and treat you to dinner, then give you a blow job, tit wank and let you do me up the bum when you get home?').

If it's the former and you're into him, you're going to have to give him a lot of reassurance – but don't go too far in case you come across as being 'Little Miss Too Good To Be True' because that's likely to confuse him. Balance up the compliments with occasional mild teasing so that he doesn't see you as a doormat.

If it's the latter, think about why you're attracted to such a man. Putting up with passive aggressive (or even plain old aggressive) behaviour suggests that you have low self-esteem and, as such, need to work on your confidence. Sure, he may have a great smile, the perfect body and fantastic bedroom technique but if his head's mixed-up then your relationship is likely to be pretty tough going. Think about whether you'd put up with such behaviour from a friend. If not, why are you prepared to put up with it from a partner? There's a strong risk that his constant negative responses will feed into your self-image and make you feel worse with every passing day. OK, you might get lucky – after a while, he might recognise what an idiot he's been and change his behaviour. But it's more likely that he'll waste your time and trash your ego. Only you can decide if that's a risk you're willing to take.

The bunny boiler

Although it's a comedy name, this is just as threatening to a man as a stalker – and can also be risky for you. When a bunny boiler wants a man, there's nothing that will stand in her way to get it and her methods of trying to convince him that she's his perfect woman know no limits. She will see any other woman entering his radar as competition and do her utmost to destroy it – which means you.

There is no reasoning with this woman. Unless you can persuade her to get psychiatric help, you'll need to either put up with her malicious behaviour, move to a new town with your man (ideally having first joined the Witness

Protection Scheme) or hope that she finds another man soon and forgets all about her ex. This may take some time. Be warned – if you stay with him, it could well be your bunny that ends up getting boiled, so unless you're really into your bloke then it may be worth deciding to move on and leave her to her petty games.

The sex goddess

So you made the mistake of asking about his ex when you were both drunk, and he admitted she was incredible in bed/a swimsuit model/a porn star. See what comes of asking questions you don't really want to know the answer to? For Christ's sake, NEVER follow this up by asking, 'Was she better than me?' Whatever the answer, the poor sod's fucked. If he says no, you won't believe him and if he says yes – well, come on, you know what your reaction will be.

The thing is, sex is about two people, not one. No matter how hot/athletic/pervy you think his ex was, he's not with her any more – he's with you. And if you're confident about your own sexuality, you can guarantee you'll be as hot as she is. You see, the secret to great sex isn't a size ten figure, 38DD breasts or an encyclopedic knowledge of the Kama Sutra. It's about chemistry, communication and feeling confident in your own skin. Get those things sorted and you'll be able to have fantastic sex too. And if he compares your technique negatively to hers? Unless it's a minor correction to your technique that you can learn from and he tells you in an incredibly sensitive way, think about whether you really want to be with such an ungentlemanly soul. Either that or begin mentioning your ex with the ten-inch penis who'd go down on you for hours (it doesn't matter if he doesn't exist – your man doesn't know that and fair's fair).

The mercy relationship

If your man goes all quiet when a certain ex's name is mentioned, don't automatically assume it means he's not over her – he may just be ashamed of himself. After all, men get just as lonely and insecure as women do, so he's just as likely to have fallen prey to a mercy relationship as you are. Generally speaking, this is one of the least threatening exes (unless she dumped him, which means he could end up questioning himself/feeling resentful towards all women because one he didn't even like had the nerve to walk out) so you don't need to worry about it. Then again, she could still be pining after him, in which case see bunny boiler on page 27.

The colleague ex

You may hate the idea of your partner working with someone he's got it on with but chances are he hates it a lot more. While you're picturing them exchanging steamy looks over the boardroom table, he's probably trying his hardest to get his deputy to go to the meeting instead of him, so that he doesn't have to face her. Honestly, unless it was a long-term relationship, his fling with a colleague is nothing to be scared of. And if it was? Start scouring the job ads for him – although chances are you'll find he's already been circling them himself.

Quiz: *It's not you, it's me*

It's all very well knowing what kind of animal you're dealing with, but it takes two people to make an ex. As such, you need to check your own behaviour to see if your ex-style is encouraging negative behaviour from your previous partners. Perhaps you obfuscate about the reasons for the break-up so much that your ex can't figure out whether he's been dumped or not and keeps harassing you with text messages (as he sees it he's just trying to contact his girlfriend). Maybe you refuse to accept that anyone who once loved you could possibly stop loving you. Or perhaps you just tune out whenever you hear something that you don't want to, then wonder why it is you're feeling so confused when you get dumped. To find out whether you're making things worse for yourself, fill in this quick quiz.

What's your ex style?

1. *How many exes are you still friends with?*
a) All of them. Just because you're not dating any more doesn't mean you shouldn't see them.
b) A few that you particularly got on with but most of the time you leave the past behind you.
c) None of them. If someone has the gall to split up with you why should you give them the pleasure of your company?

The Different Flavours of Exes

2. *How do you dump a partner you're not into?*
a) You don't – you've only ever been dumped. No matter how bad a relationship is, you'll work hard to fix things.
b) You tell them things aren't working, generally with a couple of examples of what went wrong and refuse to accept no for an answer.
c) You ignore them until they go away.

3. *How many times have you been in love?*
a) Every time you've dated anyone. That special bond between a man and a woman is sacred.
b) A few times but you've dated at least as many guys that you didn't fall for.
c) Never. You were just suckered in by wankers every time.

4. *How do you refer to your ex?*
a) Gorgeous, Mr Hot, the one that got away.
b) By their name, if you refer to them at all.
c) The bastard, needle dick, heartbreaker.

5. *How long does it take you to get over an ex?*
a) There's no such thing as over – it just hurts less than it used to.
b) It varies but usually a month or so for a short-term thing and a year or so for a long-term break-up.
c) A day, if that. Why waste time over people who don't want you?

6. *What mementos do you keep when you split up with someone?*

a) The ticket stub from your first date, the blade of grass that got stuck to your shoe the first time you went for a country walk together, a dried flower from every bunch he bought you, photos you took of him on your mobile phone when he was asleep and every gift from him, of course. Memories are precious so throwing anything away would be silly.

b) Any significant gifts and maybe a couple of photos.

c) Nothing. You burn the lot in a funeral pyre the second the relationship ends – then send him the ashes back in an envelope, along with a note telling him how over him you are.

7. *Would most of your exes recommend you as a girl-friend?*

a) Well, I keep asking them to introduce me to their fit mates but they never do.

b) Absolutely – but I probably wouldn't ask them to because it's a bit weird.

c) I'd never want to date anyone who was friends with an ex – they're clearly going to be a loser. Anyway, all my ex's mates are scared of me.

8. *What does it take for you to get 'closure' on a rela-tionship?*

a) Well, it only makes sense that you deal with any

issues as and when they arise even if it's years later. Which reminds you, you really do need to call that guy you split up with when you were 16 to tell him how much he hurt you. Again.

b) A decent talk where you can go over the major issues, in an ideal world, along with a few essential nights moaning to the girls. But if you don't get to chat to your ex, things will heal themselves in time anyway.

c) Closure, pah! The second he's out the door he's forgotten. The thoughtless, mean, ugly, tiny-dicked loser.

If you answered mostly As, you get involved way too quickly and find it unhealthily hard to let go. As such, you may find yourself getting accused of being a bunny boiler – mainly because you act like one. Sometimes, relationships just aren't meant to be. Accept it, move on and realise that just because someone's shagged you, it doesn't mean you're forever connected. No matter how lovely it may sound, your souls haven't really merged. It may well be that you like keeping your exes around to remind yourself that you're desirable but you shouldn't need constant validation to feel that way. Draw your confidence from within (yes, OK, and from your mates – it can be hard to get all your confidence from yourself) and set the exes free. Not only will it mean you've got more time to spend with your real friends but it will also make you more attractive to new men: a woman who's shagged half her male friends (as a potential new guy would see it) sets off warning bells, and you don't want your past relationships to blow your chances of having future ones. Neediness is not attractive – it may be worth seeking counselling to help you get to the bottom of why you are so insecure.

If you answered mostly Bs, you have a healthy attitude towards exes. You'll stay in contact with them if there really is a friendship worth hanging on to but you don't see the point of cluttering up your address book with the names of everyone you've ever dated. Similarly, you're honest about your feelings when a relationship ends, which means there's no excuse for an ex to get confused or clingy. So if they do, they're a twat. Carry on acting as you do, feeling safe in the knowledge that you're in the right. Don't get too smug about it though – nobody likes a smart-arse.

If you answered mostly Cs, you're a bit of a man-hater with anger issues (and then some). Dumping people by ignoring them is disrespectful and only leads to confusion (or constant pleading with you to go out with them on Friday night – because as far as they're concerned, you never split up). While this might be an easy way to boost your ego, it's hardly a mature or pleasant way to behave. You also get far too resentful about your exes. You may think this means you're over them, but in reality you're only over someone when you don't care about them at all, whether positively or negatively. Chances are that the resentment comes from insecurity. You've either had a rough family history or dated bastards and been treated badly before and thus think that men are scum – possibly both. You may well also subconsciously agree with your exes that you're not worth being with, but, because this hurts to admit to, you take it out on them instead. Look at your rage and let go of the past. Counselling could help you deal with this – chat to your GP about the options available.

Exes don't just affect the relationships that you have in a direct manner. Like it or not, every single person you go out with has an impact on who you are. They might have a relatively minor effect on you, merely introducing you to a new book or CD, teaching you how to tie a reef knot or showing you how to mix the perfect Martini. However, most significant exes will affect you on a deeper level: encouraging, even creating new neuroses or helping you get over past woes; teaching you patterns of argument or affection; making you feel better or worse about yourself. So before you can even think about having a relationship with someone else, you need to make sure your previous relationship is dealt with and neatly filed away under 'history'. It's either that or face the hellish consequences that are bound to arise if you don't.

Ten essential guidelines for dealing with your exes – and his

I. Be honest when a relationship ends so that your ex knows what the score is and doesn't have an excuse to get clingy.

2. Conversely, accept it when a partner tells you a relationship is over: trying to convince him to stay with you will just damage your self-esteem and, even if it extends the relationship for a brief amount of time, it won't ultimately work if he doesn't want to be with you.

3. Let go of any petty resentments that you had about the relationship. It's over now. There's nothing that you can do to fix the past so you're only wasting your own time.

4. Don't compare yourself to your partner's exes. He's with you, not them, and you'll only batter your own self-esteem if you waste your time doing it. It's far easier to see the good points in someone else than in yourself.

5. Only stay friends with an ex if there really is a friendship worth having. No, enjoying shagging each other when you're drunk doesn't count as friendship (but yes, OK, you are allowed to do it as long as no-one's getting hurt – except in fun ways).

6. If you meet a partner's ex when you're with him, be polite. Sniping at her will only make you look bad.

7. Limit the amount of time you think about your exes. While you can learn from past experiences, looking back at previous relationships all the time will stop you moving on into new ones.

8. If one of your partner's exes is mean to you, try to rise above it. If it keeps going on, don't whine to your man about it. Just make sure he catches his ex in the act. And if he doesn't do anything about it then, dump him.

9. Never ask a man questions about his ex that you don't really want to know the answers to, such as, 'Was she better in bed than me?'

10. Reserve a bit of gratitude for your exes and his. After all, they helped turn you into the people that you and he are today.

Chapter 2

Getting Over (or Under) an Ex

If break-ups weren't so traumatic, half of the stories in the world wouldn't have been written. From *Romeo and Juliet* to *Fatal Attraction*, *West Side Story* to *Bridget Jones's Diary*, one thing is clear: if you open yourself up to love, you're also risking pain (why do you think so many people are commitment-phobes?). But there's no reason that the pain needs to mess up your life forever. All you need to do is get over the ex and move on (a simple sentence that sums up a horribly complicated premise).

You see, like it or not, our bodies conspire against us to make splitting up hurt. When people have sex, they release oxytocin, a bonding chemical — and women release way more of it than men do. As such, we're drugged into believing that we're supposed to be with the person we're having sex with. Once you cease having access to your partner, you cut off your oxytocin source too — and it's a hard habit to break.

There are, however, numerous tricks you can use to help ease the pain. Watching soppy movies so that you can sob your heart out, pigging out on ice-cream and calling girlie mates for long self-analytical and self-obsessed chats are all good. And then there's the psychological stuff. Dull as it sounds, you need to deal with heartbreak like a grown-up.

Get over it

The first thing you need to do is accept that the relationship is over. Before you can get to this stage, chances are you'll go through the traditional five stages of grieving, as identified by Elizabeth Kubler-Ross: denial, anger, bargaining, depression and acceptance. It's easy to get stuck on any of the first four stages but you need to move through them all if you're going to move on.

Stage one: denial

In the first stage, you'll deny that you've split up – or at least that you should have done. It's common for people to withdraw from social contact at this stage, in part because it helps them maintain their own flawed version of reality. This is the stage that's likely to see you sobbing drunkenly into the phone, 'But you love me, you said you loved me, that can't just go overnight,' and other such ego-shatteringly embarrassing things. Sometimes this stage passes quickly and other times it can last for months. And months. And months.

Cruel as it sounds, this is where you need to pull yourself together. Yes, he said he loved you – but he also said he wanted to break up with you. The most recent information is the relevant information here. File the happy memories under 'nostalgia' and get on with your life. Obsessing about the past will only elongate your suffering, which is self-destructive, pointless and dull. And fixating on the future that you're no longer going to have with your ex is even more futile.

A lot of the time, when people break up they spend as much time mourning the potential future that's been blown ('But we were going to go on holiday to a desert island; we were going to call our kids Zak and India; we were going to try that sex position that needs a set of stairs to work, once we moved into a two-storey flat together; and we were going to get a puppy; and . . . and . . . and'). This is clearly a waste of your time. That future was never guaranteed. Even if you had stayed together, there's no way you could be certain that things were going to go the way that you'd talked about (just chat to someone in a long-term relationship about how many things they've planned to do with their partner but somehow never got around to doing if you want to see how true this is). If you spend time getting down about all the things you could have done together, you're extending the time that you're going to spend mourning your ex by a potentially infinite amount. And infinity is a long time to spend crying. So get a grip once you've had your initial self-indulgent wobble, otherwise it's your own life you're wasting.

Tamsin's story: I lost a year

When I split up with Angelo after ten years, I was inconsolable. We'd separated because he didn't want to get married and I did, but as soon as I ended things I realised that I just wanted to be with him, married or not. Sadly, he wouldn't take me back.

I spent the whole of that summer staying in; I only left the house to go to work. My mates tried to drag me out but I couldn't face it. I reread the letters he'd sent me and looked through our picture albums again and again.

Getting through my first Christmas without him was even worse. We'd always had big celebrations together. That year he didn't even send me a card. I spent the day in bed, alone.

When New Year rolled round, I grudgingly agreed to go out with my best friend. I'd been out of the social scene for so long that I felt like an alien surrounded by all these people, who used to be my friends. But as the alcohol flowed and I relaxed, I started to enjoy myself. I even got a bit flirty with one cute guy. Nothing happened other than a kiss at midnight but I realised I'd been cocooning myself for too long. It was hard, but I decided to pack up all the things that reminded me of my ex and redecorated my flat for a fresh start. I still have the occasional pang of missing him but I can cope with it now. I realised that, trite as it sounds, life is for living, not mourning.

Stage two: anger

When you admit you have actually broken up, you'll probably move onto stage two – anger. At this point you may well believe that you're totally over 'the bastard'. If you get to hear about what he's up to – say, you learn that he's been dumped by the girl he left you for – you'll possibly pepper your conversations with anecdotes about things that have gone wrong for him, and how pleased you are that he's suffering because he deserves it. You may even consider seeking revenge (don't actually do it though – revenge lacks class and even though it can sometimes be funny, you'll end up regretting it once your sanity returns). Your friends, who've already had to suffer hours of you sobbing down the phone at them, will now get dragged into long conversations about your ex's tiny penis, boring cunnilingus techniques or particularly odorous farts. If you hear your ex is dating anyone else, she may well get caught in the crossfire of your anger and end up being referred to as 'the slut' (or at least have her buttocks size commented upon negatively). The thing is, if you're feeling angry at your ex, you're still feeling something, and, sad as it is, until you feel nothing (other than the occasional hit of nostalgia) you're not over him. So you need to wade through the hurt and frustration in order to move on to the next stage. Kick-boxing classes may help.

Alyson's story: I barred him from my life

Bruce was a mid-20s surfer-type who worked at my local pub and was popular with everyone, so when he asked me out, I couldn't help but feel smug. He'd chosen me over all the 20-something trendy, leggy blondes in the bar. I'd just turned 40, so I was blown away that he was interested in me.

We dated for a few months and I had fun – even if, to be honest, he didn't have that much to say and wasn't particularly good in bed. After a while I tried to dump him but he got really upset so I said I'd stay with him. A week later, he dumped me – during his cigarette break! I was outraged. How could *he* dump *me*? We'd had a chance to have an amicable break-up and he'd blown it because he was so egotistical that he couldn't let me be the one to end it.

From that point onwards, I stopped going to his bar and told all my friends to give it a wide berth too. It was a pain because he worked at the best bar in the area but, being loyal, my friends did as I asked.

I ranted about him for months, and when I heard he was dating a 20-year-old PR called Jemima it was the last straw. It wasn't that I was in love with him but how could he move on from intelligent conversation with me to some fluffy-bunny type?

Then one day I saw them together. We were polite to each other but when I got home I had to have a gin and tonic. For some reason, seeing him in the flesh made me realise things really were over – even though

I didn't want him back. He didn't matter all that much and there was no need to be cross with him – he was just a weak man who wasn't right for me and if I was honest with myself, there was no way that things would have worked anyway.

I stopped obsessing about him and told my mates they could drink wherever they wanted. I haven't gone back to his bar yet but that's more because I don't want to see him flirting with other women – I'm still not strong enough to handle that. But one day I will be.

Stage three: bargaining

Stage three is where it gets really good fun: you start bargaining. It could be a case of praying (even if you've never been in a church before in your life), swearing that you'll give up smoking, chocolate, drinking and masturbation if only you can get your ex back (trust me, no man is worth that level of sacrifice). It might be that you decide to make yourself over, physically, emotionally or both, in the hope that if you correct all the 'flaws' your ex saw in you, he'll take you back. Anything and everything will become an excuse for why you split up, and you'll feel certain you can fix things with your ex 'if only…'

If you want to keep any dignity at all, for Christ's sake never bargain with your ex in person. It won't work and it will annihilate your self-esteem faster than being told you're 'not bad looking, for a fat girl'. Instead, you need to realise that no matter what, your relationship is over. Yes, even if you did kill every other woman in the world and were your ex's only hope of repopulating the planet.

Well, maybe not then but scoring that much cyanide is only going to get you into trouble, and he'll think you're a bit of a psycho. As such, you're not ever going to get back together. Sorry. Still, plenty more fish in the sea, eh?

Aisha's story: I'd do anything for love

William and I broke up because he said I wasn't stylish enough for him. Rather than deciding he was a thoughtless and arrogant knob (as I now know he is) I decided to become fashionable so that he'd love me again. I spent a fortune on women's magazines and educated myself about all the latest looks. Then I called up my most fashion-conscious friend and we went shopping together. I had my hair cut, got a make-over and turned up at a party he was going to be at, dressing in my new finery of course.

It was a disaster. He didn't even say hello when I walked in, and when I went up to chat to him, he didn't comment on my clothes. He was too busy leching over some size six model-type. I realised that changing my look wasn't going to get back this vain, self-centred man. On the plus side, I do have a fab new wardrobe and a new-found interest in clothes, so it wasn't a complete waste of time.

Stage four: depression

After all the bargaining comes the realisation that no matter what you do, it's just not going to work. At this point, it's pretty likely that you'll get sad – possibly even depressed. You may feel numb, even though anger and sadness are still lurking beneath the surface, waiting to pounce on you during the 4 am terrors. Don't let the blahs take you. Get out and exercise, talk to friends (by now, they're no doubt bored of hearing about your ex and you could probably do with focusing your mind on something else, so try to spend at least some of the time talking about them rather than yourself). Eat healthily, get a good night's sleep (when you're not out having fun) and pamper yourself. Don't mask the depression with alcohol, drugs or casual sex – it'll only make you feel more hellish – save them for when you're feeling perky (except for the drugs because they're naughty, and if you get caught you'll find your pulling options reduced to just the other people in prison with you, which is limiting).

Mimi's story: Medication helped me through

I thought that Jack and I would be together forever – we'd even named our (unborn) babies – so it came as a shock to me when he dumped me because 'things just weren't working out'. I hadn't realised that there was anything wrong with us. As a result, I plunged into a horrible, dark place.

I had a history of depression when I was in my early teens and recognised a lot of the same feelings coming back. I was determined not to let depression get a grip on me again though, particularly not over a man, so I went to the doctors and explained the problem. My GP was really understanding and put me on a course of Prozac. I ended up taking it for six months.

It didn't stop me from crying over Jack but it did mean that I didn't become suicidal – something I was genuinely scared of. When I came off the pills, enough time had passed for me to feel better about things, so it was easier for me to cope with. I wouldn't hesitate to do the same thing again, if anyone broke my heart – not that I'm looking for a man right now.

Stage five: acceptance

And finally – and it will probably feel like the ending of an epic saga by the time it kicks in – there's acceptance. You accept that your ex is an ex. You don't want to get him back and you don't want to kill him. Congratulations! You're officially 'over the bastard'. Enjoy some time being single before plunging back into the whole relationship thing again, and remind yourself what you're like when you're not all heartbroken. See, you're quite nice really, aren't you?

But what if you still haven't reached the acceptance stage? Don't worry, there are a few tricks you can pull to help yourself move on more quickly.

Speeding up the process

Although you have to let time work its magic, there are various things you can do to help you get through the five stages that bit faster. From a practical point of view, you can speed the healing process along by getting any significant milestones out of the way as soon as possible. Return each other's belongings straight away. This doesn't include presents you've bought each other – that's just petty. However, to get all feng shui on you, the longer your ex's belongings clutter up your house, the longer they'll clutter up your mind. In addition, you don't want to have extra reasons to think of your ex when you're looking around for your favourite top and realise that it's still at his flat. You'll probably have enough excuses to think about him during this stage, without creating any more.

After returning each other's belongings, the next stage (assuming there aren't kids involved) is to cease contact and delete your ex's phone number from your mobile phone. Otherwise, you'll only be tempted to drunken dial – an action that never has a positive outcome (unless you're a drama queen/like desperate inebriated sex). If you've managed to memorise your ex's number, try to unmemorise it (harder than it sounds). And learn from your mistake: in future, never learn a man's phone number by heart – it'll only come back to haunt you should you split up.

It doesn't matter if you want to stay friends with your ex, you still need to cease all contact when you first split up, until you've fully recovered from the relationship. Only once you get to that stage will you even remotely be able to be friends with someone that you once loved. Clinging desperately onto some semblance of contact will only make things harder. As a rough guide, you need at least a month without contact to get over a short (six months or fewer) relationship, and a minimum of three months without contact to get over a long-term relationship. It may sound like an impossible feat, particularly if you're used to seeing someone every day, but it's by far the easiest way to heal your broken heart.

If you've been together for any significant amount of time, there are other milestones that are harder to deal with quickly: your first Christmas apart, first birthday alone and the first anniversary of your break-up. The easiest way to cope with these is by keeping yourself occupied. Arrange to do something fun so that you're distracted from moping around the house, crying into your cat and swearing you'll never be happy again. You could even try having an 'universary' celebration – celebrating the first year apart from your ex. A massive party is probably a bit much – you don't want to turn it into a bigger deal than it is – but a night out with a girlie mate or a weekend away somewhere you love can serve as a handy reminder both that life does go on and that you are in a better place than you were when you first broke up. Like it or not, you will survive.

Julia's story: My seaside holiday washed away the pain

I'd been with Wayne for seven years so when we split up because he cheated on me, I was devastated. I spent the first three months after we broke up in bed pretty much the whole time that I wasn't working, and it took a huge amount of support from my friends for me to finally drag myself out of my depression.

A year after we split up, a friend commented on how much happier I seemed now that I was single. After the initial agony, I'd got on with my life and found that I was a lot more motivated. Wayne hadn't been particularly social and he'd dragged me down to his level, so we'd spent most of the time in our house watching DVDs or playing computer games. Now I went to the gym twice a week, had started Japanese classes and had a lot more time to see my friends.

I realised that what my friend had said was right, and decided there and then that I wanted to thank her for helping me open my eyes. As a token of my appreciation, I offered to take her to the seaside for the day, all expenses paid. She was surprised but flattered and willingly accepted my offer. We had a great day that still holds many happy memories for me, and I still think of it as the day that I really finally got over Wayne.

Sadly, 'no man is an island', so it's not always just your ex you have to deal with when a relationship ends. If you've been with a partner for a long time, there's a strong chance that you'll have shared friendship groups, belongings or even the same home. You might love his family or he might be a surrogate son to your parents. If so, you need to deal with each issue individually.

Belongings and a home are by far the easiest to deal with – after all, they're just tangible things. In the case of the former, divide the belongings fairly between you and if there are any mutual items you can't agree over, sell them and split the money. With a home, set a 'moving out' date for one or both of you so that it doesn't become a never-ending situation. If possible, take it in turns to spend the weekend (or longer) with friends so you see as little of each other as possible. And it should go without saying but for goodness' sake, don't share a bed with each other. Even if you don't have much space, an airbed is inexpensive and can fit in the smallest flat.

If you're going to stay in the home that you lived in with your ex once he's gone, make sure that you have a thorough clear-out when he leaves. If you have enough space, swap round the rooms of the house so that the living room becomes your bedroom or the office becomes the dining room. That way you'll help shift the memories that are lodged in your surroundings. And burn some incense or scented candles to change the smell of your flat. Smell is the most primal sense and, as such, is likely to trigger memories of your ex, so don't let him get up your nose. Invite your girlie mates round to help clear out your flat. If you play your favourite music and have a glass of wine, you're less likely to end up sobbing over the battered teddy you find behind the sofa that he gave you on your first date. Hell, you might even end up having fun.

When it comes to dealing with mutual friends, one easy rule is that the person who first met that friend is the one to 'keep' them, though obviously it depends on the depth of the friendship – if one of you is an acquaintance and the other is 'best mates' with said person, the 'best mate' is obviously more important. In the case of friends that you made together, you'll have to share. Agree with your ex that you'll both avoid talking negatively about each other and that you'll warn each other if you're going to a social occasion you're both likely to be invited to. But generally, you need to accept you'll probably lose some friends at the end of a long-term relationship. While it is possible for you both to stay friends with the same people, it's likely to be awkward, particularly in the early stages of the break-up. Your friends may feel that you want them to take sides, or feel guilty for still liking your ex. And if you keep the same friendship group, it's more likely you'll run into your ex, which will only prolong your heartbreak. Get out and find some new friends to go with your new life. It will help you move on.

With family, it's another loss you'll both have to suffer. If your folks love your ex, explain to them that it hurts you to see him, that you've had to sever contact to get over him and you don't want him to see them either, as it's too much of a reminder of the past. Tell your ex too, so he doesn't wonder why your mum's suddenly giving him the cold shoulder in the supermarket. Conversely, no matter how much you love your ex's mum, her baby boy has to come first. Don't nip round there to cry on her shoulder or call her for updates on him. If you're still speaking to a man's family, you're keeping yourself tied to him, which will make it harder for you to heal. Once you've both got over your heartbreak you may be able to resume the relationships you had with each other's families, but not before.

If you have kids together it's tougher. Indeed, it's such a minefield that it could fill a book on its own. Obviously you can't sever contact with your ex entirely, as that will make the children suffer. However, you can minimise contact, at least at first. Be civil to your partner in front of the children if you do have to see him – say, on a visit – but don't use the children as an excuse to see him. It's manipulative and damaging to everyone concerned. Don't let the kids see that you're unhappy about speaking to your partner. However, in the early days it may be worth asking your parents to pick the kids up and drop them off when you're exchanging custody. A bit of space will help give you some perspective and in time you'll be able to form a new relationship – as 'parents' rather than 'exes'.

Regardless of the losses, with any luck and a bit of self-awareness, you'll work your way through the hell that is breaking up and be ready to move on. Sometimes it'll take a few days, sometimes months, sometimes years. And no matter what you do, there's always the risk that you might have some baggage lingering around to trip you up when you get into your next relationship.

The quick and dirty approach

Of course, going through all that lot is the sensible thing to do, but there is another option – which some may say is ill-advised. As one woman who was interviewed for the book said, the easiest way to get over an ex is to 'Find a new love and wank more.' However, this is only a 'plastering over the cracks' solution that will temporarily abate the pain. And if you make a habit of it, there's a risk you'll end up building up a backlog of baggage that's way harder to deal with than suffering each of the recovery stages immediately after the relationship ends. But sometimes, a quick and dirty solution is all that you feel capable of doing.

If you do go off and have sex with someone else, it will give you a new burst of oxytocin, keeping your supply at its previous levels. It has numerous downsides though – all you need to do is spend a night in the pub sharing rebound stories with your mates and you'll hear all about them. But as a brief recap, in all likelihood your judgement will be clouded by your 'drug-led' desire (or low self-esteem) if you go for a rebound shag. Because you're in a vulnerable state, there's the risk you might have unprotected sex (for heaven's sake, please don't), which exposes you to all manner or other nasties. The new oxytocin hit doesn't last that long and if you get rejected again, you'll probably sink even lower. It's also a tad immature – not to mention unfair on your rebound shag. If you pick this option, make sure that your sex partner knows that it's just a fling rather than anything serious – you don't want your old relationship to end up hurting anyone other than the people who were in it.

Baggage reclaim

It doesn't matter how secure and mature you are, after the break-up of a heavy relationship it's only human to have a bit of baggage cluttering up your psyche. It takes time to get rid of it, even after you've dealt with every last vestigial pangs of love. If you find yourself thinking any of the following, you may well be carrying something with you that would be much better left behind:

I'm so undesirable that no-one will ever want me

If you go out with a guy who doesn't put out, it's very easy to fall into the trap of believing it's because of a flaw in yourself rather than merely mismatched libidos. This is particularly likely to happen if you were always the one to initiate sex and found that you got the answer 'no' far more than you got your jollies.

It's not unusual, should you pick up this particular piece of baggage, for you to suddenly become rampantly sexual, willingly copulating with anyone who offers simply because they've asked, regardless of whether you find them attractive. You may find yourself constantly seeking sexual validation: wearing outrageous clothes, drinking and taking drugs to excess to fuel a 'party girl' personality and flirting with anyone who's legally old enough (or far too old but can do the job given enough Viagra).

Although a wild year can be useful for some people, particularly after a long and staid relationship ends, if this behaviour goes on for too long it can become destructive.

Getting Over (or Under) an Ex

You may find yourself believing that the only reason someone could possibly like you is for sex, or get depressed if you go out and you don't pull.

Instead, remind yourself that your ex's lack of sex drive said far more about him than it does about you. Men can suffer from low libidos because of stress, excessive drink or drug use, an unhealthy diet, depression and a multitude of other reasons. There are so many causes for low libido that the odds that it was because you're not sexy are really pretty slim. More to the point, you've split up with him now. The world isn't made up of clones of your ex so every other man out there isn't going to be as averse to getting it on with you as he was. But you don't need to do it with all of them to prove this.

The problem with having this belief lurking in your subconscious once you're in a relationship is that you're likely to treat your partner like a knight in shining armour, clinging on to him so tightly that his armour gets dented. This is an easy way to make a man leap right back onto his horse and ride off, alone, into the sunset.

Alternatively, you may get hyper-sensitive towards rejection, having a go at your man the first time he says that he's too tired for sex, for fear that you'll end up in the same state as you did with your ex.

Either way, you need to let go of the past. Separate your new man from your old man in your head – they are not the same person and it's unfair to blame Mr New for everything that Mr Old did (or, more accurately, didn't do). And masturbate more often. It's a good way to keep those 'gagging for it' pangs at bay. Plus, it's fun.

I wasted my youth on my ex and now I'm too old to find love

This is a myth. OK, you might have spent your teens, 20s, 30s or 40s with a guy who turned out not to be Mr Right but that doesn't mean you were wasting your youth. It's pretty damned likely that, while dating this man, you were also going out with friends, working and having other experiences that helped shape you into the person you are today. Having a relationship is only one small part of life, not the reason for living. So let go of the resentment and accept that it's better to be single than being with a man who isn't right for you.

As for the 'too old to find love' fear? It's nonsense. Sure, it might seem tougher meeting a guy the older you get but that's because you're getting choosier, so the one you end up with – should someone good enough come along – will be far more suited to you than your ex. Women of all ages find partners every day – just look at the amount of times Joan Collins has been married. If you go around obsessing that you're too old to get a partner then you'll project a negative state of mind that's hardly sexy and *then* you won't pull. But if you accept that you'll meet someone who's right for you when the time is right, chill out and enjoy life, you'll be much happier and far more likely to find a man.

If, instead, you carry this baggage into a relationship with you then it's all too likely that you'll end up going out with someone inappropriately young in order to validate yourself, or someone that you don't really fancy, because you're so grateful that they were prepared to 'take you on'. Even if you don't fall into either of these traps, you could still turn into 'Please Impregnate Me' woman, with your biological clock's alarm set to go off at any second. This is not a good look, and is liable to scare off even the nicest man, so calm the hell down. Babies are not the centre of the universe. And anyway, women can have babies later and later nowadays due to advances in medical science. Stop racing for the happy ending and just enjoy life for what it is right now.

No man is trustworthy

If your ex cheated on you, lied to you or left you for someone else, it's all too easy to believe that every other man will be like him. Bollocks. You just got unlucky – and chances are you can spot the warning signs a lot quicker now you've had the experience of dating a swine.

The big thing to be wary of with this particular piece of baggage is not to let it turn you into a paranoid man-hater. If you find yourself suspecting every man you date is cheating on you, for reasons as tissue-paper thin as,'He chatted to the check-out girl for longer than I would when he was getting the shopping,' then you'll find that they will.

By spending your entire relationship getting jealous about your bloke's every move, you'll encourage him to think, 'May as well be hung for a sheep as a lamb', and stray. No-one likes getting told off, least of all for something they haven't done, so don't act like a possessive nightmare and it's much more likely that you won't get cheated on again. If you really can't get over your ex's cheating then the only other option is to switch teams and start dating women – and unless you fancy them, that's really not a good choice to make.

I'm a nightmare to go out with

All too often, perfectly sane and rational women will absorb negative comments made in a relationship and believe them to be true. As such, if an ex has told you that you're hard work, you'll believe it. OK, there may be some semblance of truth in this or, more likely, it could just be that you and your ex were a mismatch. Well, you've split up now. That nightmare is over. You can move on to having sweet dreams with another relationship instead.

Whatever you do, avoid listing all your nightmarish qualities to any new men you end up dating. If you point things out so negatively they'll start looking for the bad signs and will undoubtedly find things that tie in with what you say – whether they're there or not – rather than just judging you for the person that you are. Why shoot yourself in the foot? You're not a nightmare to go out with. At least not any more than any other woman.

Bin the baggage

No matter what baggage you've acquired, one of the biggest problems with it is that, unless it's resolved, it can be all too easy to collect a matching luggage set to go with it. You date one bloke who gives you grief, end the relationship and swear that you'll never make the same mistake again, only to find yourself in exactly the same situation when your next relationship comes along. The details may change – where one man might not commit because he's an alcoholic, another might not commit because he's married – but the underlying issue is the same. Therapist Emma Gold explains:

> According to Freud, we are often compelled to repeat patterns of behaviour whereby we revisit, remember and work through memories that have been repressed in order to gain mastery over them.

This means that it can be all too easy to fall into a pattern of negative behaviour. If you find yourself constantly dating 'unavailable' men – whether emotionally or merely 'off limits' (say, married to someone else) – it suggests that, however subconsciously, you're playing a part in your own negative experiences.

If you have such a long string of exes that Freddy Kreuger is starting to look like a good relationship choice, or you think that your baggage could be affecting your love life, there's a good chance that you need to work through your issues. Otherwise you may find yourself trapped in a loop, making the same mistakes for the rest of your life. For example, if you find relationships a struggle, it could be because you had your heart broken when you were younger and subconsciously don't want to risk getting hurt again. Or there could be something even deeper at play. Gold continues:

> Like many psychotherapists, I believe that we are drawn
> to partners who reflect or express unacknowledged

parts of ourselves. So, if we apparently inexplicably find ourselves with angry men, I am willing to bet that there is a great well of untapped anger lurking beneath our own surface. Similarly, women who are ambivalent about relationships tend to find men who are more overt about wanting to remain unattached.

Sadly, there's no easy solution — you need to tackle your own insecurities and flaws. It's all too easy to fall into playing the blame game, excusing your lack of relationship success on the basis that 'all men are bastards' because it's easier than getting to grips with the problems that lurk within your own psyche. Gold says,

> The journey of self-discovery, whilst rocky, is ultimately less painful, however, since we are dealing with reality rather than fantasy.

Tough as it may be to hear, a failed relationship is about two people, not one. Even if your ex was rude, grumpy and dull, you were attracted to him in the first place, which makes you complicit in however the relationship played out. But on the plus side, it's a lot easier to fix yourself than change a man into the person you want him to be, even if it does take guts to admit you're not perfect.

Only once you've got all the emotional baggage out of the way can you even think about forming a healthy relationship with someone new, so it's worth making the effort to sort yourself out. If you find any baggage particularly hard to shift on your own, don't be scared to seek counselling to help you lose it. A few hours of therapy could well be all you need to help you dump those suitcases full of negative bullshit. This will leave you with both hands free to grab at all the hot men that cross your path – or hold onto the one that you've got. If you don't sort out that baggage, there's always the risk that you may feel tempted back into your ex's life.

Exes and friendship

So is it ever healthy to stay friends with an ex? Although it may seem mature and sophisticated, it can also be clingy and rife with complications. If you're friends, you'll have to smile sweetly when he starts dating someone else – and he'll know when you meet someone new. Either that or you'll find yourself treading on eggshells, trying desperately to avoid saying something that may inadvertently upset the other one.

Staying friends can also be a way of keeping feelings going – you want to be with a partner, he doesn't want to be with you so you 'settle' for friendship as a poor second. If this is the case, break away. As you already know, you need to get over an ex before you can be friends with him. Still not sure whether you're over the ex? If you baulk at the idea of telling him that you're dating someone else or cry at the thought of him dating another woman then it's a clear sign that you're not ready for it yet – and possibly never will be. As a general rule, it's much easier to be friends with an ex once you've spent some time apart and ideally dated – or at least had sex with – someone else.

If you do decide to try to remain friends with an ex, you need to be fully aware of what to expect – namely, if you're lucky, a friendship. Being friends with an ex is not an excuse for you to rehash everything that went wrong in your relationship ad nauseum. It doesn't mean that you were destined to be together and need some time to get to know each other better. It just means that you've got a new friend.

Barbara's story: My friendships fluctuate

I tend to stay friends with my exes but I wouldn't say that we're constantly close to each other. When they're single, things tend to be mutually flirty. When they're attached, I help check out whether the woman they're seeing is worth it in the early days, and help them through any relationship issues when things move on. And if their girlfriends get iffy about me I fade into the background – most of my exes are so strong-willed that I know those kinds of relationships won't last long anyway and they'll either be back as a mate or will settle down with 'the one', in which case I'm more than happy to let things go. Love's the most important thing, after all.

Somehow, my relationship with exes seems natural. I'll admit it's nice when we're single at the same time as we can both get a bit of saucy chat and feel better about ourselves, but even when it's just a friends thing, I like having them in my life. It means that I get to see how they behave in relationships in general. This has certainly helped teach me about the way to behave with men, because they're really honest with me about the things their girlfriends do that are a big mistake.

If you're unsure about whether you're ready to be friends, chances are, you're not. One good test is to think about your response to your ex in various potentially compromising situations – say, flirting with one of your friends, turning up late to meet you or going on holiday with a new partner. Does it annoy or upset you more than it would with a friend who isn't an ex? If so, you're not nearly over your ex enough to build a solid friendship, and you need to give yourself more time.

It's also worth examining why you want to be friends with your ex. Some women are so insecure that once they've had a relationship, they can't let it go. They need to stay in contact with everyone they've ever dated to remind themselves that they're good enough to date. It should go without saying that this is negative and self-destructive behaviour. You don't need to keep your exes around like hunting trophies. You had some time together. It ended. Move on. The only reason to stay friends with an ex is if you genuinely have enough in common that there are proper foundations to form a friendship.

Good foundations for friendship

- Common hobbies and interests.
- A similar sense of humour.
- A shared taste in books, music, films or all three.
- Entertaining conversation.
- Mutual trust, affection and respect.

Bad foundations for friendship

- Lust.
- Convenience (say, a shared friendship group – or worse, a flat. Move out, or kick him out, for the sake of your sanity).
- Loneliness.
- Desperation.
- A need to prove that you're not the person that your ex thinks you are.

Janie's story: I love having him in my life

Alexander and I had a brief but extremely intense relationship last year. He was a big party animal though, and after a few months, even though I was convinced that he was 'the one' and wanted us to get married one day, I just couldn't cope with his lifestyle. He was out every night – drinking, taking drugs and getting into weird and wonderful situations. I never knew what was going to happen when we were out, which was exciting at first, but soon became awkward as he wouldn't tone down his behaviour. This was really tough as I was going through a rough patch in my life and needed a boyfriend who I could just talk to and get hugs from.

The spilt from him was one of the worst I've ever had, even though I initiated it. One minute we'd try to stay friends, the next we'd be rowing about something that had happened when we were dating, so eventually we drifted apart. Then, out of the blue, he got called into his boss's office and told he had to tone down his lifestyle or he was going to get the sack. He loves his job, and had begun to realise how much of a liability his behaviour was making him, so decided it was worth the sacrifice.

Most of his friends were from the party scene, so he called me to help support him through it. Straight, he was a different person. We got into the habit of chatting most nights so I could remind him why he shouldn't go out partying (at his behest) and now, five months later, I'd describe him as one of my best friends. I did harbour an urge for us to get back together for a while, but he's got a policy of 'never go back', so there's no point. Once I realised this, I let go of the past. Now we never get into rows about the relationship we had. In a way it feels like two different people dated each other because these days we talk and play Scrabble rather than drinking and having wild sex – but I'm glad we stayed friends.

Should your initial friendship with an ex develop into a firm friendship, you still need to be very aware of potential complications. You'd think it'd get easier once you'd been friends with an ex for a while but this isn't always the case. As you learn more about your ex through the friendship, you may find yourself becoming drawn to them romantically all over again – or vice versa. If this happens you also run the risk of repeating the heartbreak.

If you're friends with an ex, and you start to develop romantic feelings for them after you thought you'd got over them, it's important that you communicate rather than feeling hopeful that every glance or casual touch is loaded with meaning. Even if you think that your ex feels the same way that you do, you may just be misinterpreting their friendly gesture as a sign that they're falling back in love with you. As such, you need to check that you're on the same page before you get yourself into a situation in which they could hurt you again. Splitting up with a partner is bad enough: ceasing contact when you've failed even to be friends can be even harder on your ego. Similarly, if you think an ex who's a friend is falling for you again, you need to front up to them about it and tell them the truth. It may seem harsh but it's a lot fairer than letting them get head over heels about someone who's not going to return their feelings.

Friendships with exes have a huge potential for being destructive. You may find yourself holding back from dating other people because you're subconsciously (or consciously) hoping that your ex will see how great you are as a friend and fall for you as a lover. You might find yourself rowing with your ex about people you date because they're jealous, either of the person you're dating or of you because you've moved on. You might feel down when you hear about your ex's new girlfriend – because obviously, as a friend, they'll talk to you about their romantic life. So remember, unless you really do have the basis of a solid and life-enhancing friendship, it's really not worth complicating things and opening yourself up to stress by staying friends with exes.

Sally's story: He got me down

I really missed Erik when we stopped seeing each other so when he got in touch a few months later, asking me out for a drink and saying that he missed my company, I leapt at the chance. I thought that he was feeling the same as I was and wanted me back.

That night, I realised that he only wanted to be friends – he'd been a fairly amorous boyfriend so when he didn't make a move on me or respond to any of my moves, I knew there was no chance of things getting back to the way they were. But I kidded myself into thinking that I didn't mind. After all, I still got to see him and hang out with him – and that was surely mostly what I'd missed?

I hadn't predicted how jealous I'd end up getting. Erik's a good-looking guy and he attracts a lot of women. I didn't really realise how many until he started telling me – as a friend – all about his conquests. I didn't feel I could complain about it because that's normal 'mate' behaviour, but I often found myself feeling annoyed or resentful when I got home at the end of the night after seeing him.

After a month of his boring stories, I'd had enough. I stopped answering his calls because I didn't see why I should have to listen to him talking about other women and making me feel bad. Oddly enough, I didn't miss him at all this time round. I guess I just needed to see what he was really like: shallow, obsessed with the chase and really nothing special.

Quiz: Should you stay friends with your ex?

Of course, even if you know something's a bad idea it can be very tempting to do it, so fill in this quiz, ticking the option that's closest to your feelings, to see if you're able to stay friends with your ex and check whether it's really a good idea.

1. *You would say that:*
a) You're still in love with your ex.
b) They're still in love with you.
c) You split up because neither of you were in love with each other.
d) There's chemistry between you and your ex but you don't love each other.

2. *If you walked into a bar with a new partner and saw your ex with someone new:*
a) You'd feel sad he was with someone else.

b) You'd feel guilty if he saw you with someone else.
c) You'd feel a bit weird but you'd both be polite to each other and move on.
d) You'd want all the details.

3. *You meet someone who'd get on well with your ex as a potential partner. You would:*
a) Try to keep them away from him.
b) Introduce them and pray they like each other.
c) Mention them to your ex the next time you see him.
d) Try to line up a threesome.

4. *The last time you cried about your ex was:*
a) Last night.
b) When he phoned you 17 times in a row.
c) A few days after you split up.
d) When he gave you a fantastic orgasm that left tears streaming down your face.

5. *Your ex cancels seeing you last minute. Do you:*
a) Feel really hurt.
b) Feel relieved.
c) Feel a bit put out but no big deal.
d) Get your vibrator out.

6. *If you imagine marrying your ex you:*
a) Feel blissfully happy and have mentally planned out everything from what you'll wear to the catering.

b) Have nightmares, knowing that he must have drugged you to get you down the aisle.

c) Laugh.

d) Start planning all the dirty things you could do on the honeymoon, at the same time as researching quickie divorce lawyers.

7. *You see a book, CD or novelty you think your ex would like. Do you:*

a) Buy it immediately and send it in the post first-class or hand-deliver it wearing your sexiest frock.

b) Walk away quickly in case he's anywhere in the area.

c) Mention it to him the next time you see him.

d) Buy it for him with plans to trade it for sexual favours.

8. *When you think about your previous relationship with your ex, you:*

a) Lose yourself in daydreams then cry when you realise it's ended.

b) Wonder how it happened in the first place and what the hell you were thinking.

c) Have a few nostalgic pangs but see it as the past.

d) Get your vibrator out.

If you answered mostly As, there's no way in hell that you should see this man as a friend. You're in love with him and desperately want him back so you'll be a rubbish mate to him and you'll get your self-esteem crushed into the bargain. Step away from the man.

If you answered mostly Bs, you probably don't want to be friends with him anyway but if you do, beware — he's likely to turn crazy on you. The guy's still besotted. Move on — at speed.

If you answered mostly Cs, you're in the perfect situation to be mates. There's affection, you enjoy each other's company and there are no heavy emotions floating around the place. Get in there.

And if you answered mostly Ds, you don't miss the man, you miss his meat. Get a room. Now. You're leaving wet patches.

Forming a healthy relationship with your ex

So, now you know whether you should be friends or not, there's the small matter of how exactly to do it. It might seem simple enough — hang out, talk nonsense, be mates — but it can be far more complex than a 'normal' friendship.

To start with, if there are any lingering resentments hanging over you, spend one evening having them out so that your friendship can progress. Agree to do this without attributing blame — it's just about clearing the air. If one or both of you is the remotest bit temperamental, writing each other letters then exchanging them face to face, or sending a carefully written email, can be an easier way to manage this without things getting heated. Don't let the issues escalate – simply answer any questions that are asked honestly and as unemotionally as you can. Until you've sorted any problems left over from the relationship, they'll always be lurking there at the back of your mind, waiting to kibosh the friendship. Once you've had this conversation, agree to draw a line under the past. You were once boyfriend and girlfriend. You're now friends. Your romantic entanglement was a separate and different relationship that has no bearing on the friendship you're now forming.

Sarah's story: We have a code

Robert and I had a fantastic relationship but it all fell apart when he had to go travelling for six months. He told me honestly that he didn't think he'd be able to stay faithful to me so, even though I was upset, we split up but promised to remain friends.

To begin with, it was hard, particularly when he mentioned seeing other girls. Then I mentioned a guy I'd started dating and my ex said he had a 'twinge' of jealousy. I admitted I'd felt the same way when he'd talked about girls, but we both agreed it'd be wrong to get back together. Instead, we now stop each other if a conversation's painful and admit to having a 'twinge'. It feels like a safe way to admit that we still have feelings for each other and stops us from getting annoyed with each other and sniping instead.

Given the complexities of staying friends with an ex, it can also be a good idea to artificially instigate a way to deal with any potential jealousies between you. Even if you're both over each other it's not that uncommon for people to feel insecure once their ex starts dating another person.

One way to avoid this is with some pre-emptive action. When you first become friends, go out on the pull together so that you're firmly establishing yourselves as being independent parties. Agree that you're there purely for casual flirtation and number exchanging, and that whatever happens, you'll leave the venue together so that neither of you is stuck on your own trying to find a cab at midnight. Other than that, leave each other to it when one of you is on the prowl. You can compare notes in between flirting, but not scupper each other's chances.

It may sound hard but, if you can prove to yourself (and each other) that you're emotionally strong enough to cope with seeing your ex chatting up someone else, you'll lessen the chances of any jealousies cropping up at a later date when one of you meets someone with real relationship potential. More to the point, if it turns out that neither of you are capable of dealing with it, you'll know you're not ready to be friends yet and can avoid the more complicated potential future issue of having to choose between an ex who's become a friend, and a new partner.

Emma's story: It was easier than I thought it would be

When I first went out to a party with Ian I thought it would be hard to watch him flirt with other girls. We'd been together for about six months, which is a long time for me. As it was, there was a really cute guy at the party. He started chatting to me quite early on and it was only a few hours later when I realised that Ian was looking at his watch, bored. He hadn't been as lucky as me, and the woman he'd tried to pull had left. I have to admit I felt a bit smug when I told him I wouldn't be going home with him that night. Well, he was the one who dumped me.

Honesty is another essential ingredient of staying friends with an ex, particularly when it comes to your love life. You need to tell them if you start dating someone else, regardless of how uncomfortable it may feel at first. Don't go into all the graphic details (save those for your girlie mates) and don't compare the new partner to your ex (it'd drive you mad if they did it to you). Just let them know if there's something significant happening in your romantic life at the earliest possible stage, so that they have time to process it – and ask them to do the same with you.

If you deal with any baggage and jealousy, make sure that you tell each other the truth and don't let your expectations get out of control, then there's a good chance you'll be able to maintain a firm friendship with your ex. And if you're lucky, before too long you'll forget you ever dated and just enjoy the friendship for what it is.

Tina's story: I don't know what I saw in him

I went out with Jason from age 20 to 28 so he was a fairly important part of my life. He was the first man I had sex with, the first man I fell in love with and the first man who broke my heart. We split up because he said he didn't think it was a good idea to only be with one person for the whole of your life. I'd thought we were going to grow old together but, after we'd split up and I'd got over the initial pain, I began to see he was right. I started dating different people, while still staying in contact with Jason (though only as friends). I began to realise what a fuddy-duddy Jason had been. He wasn't very experimental and we always ended up doing the same things: cinema on a Saturday, football on a Sunday (me watching, him play-ing) and sitting watching TV every other day of the week. My life got a lot more interesting after we split.

I also realised that there were much hotter men out there than Jason. I fancied him when I first met him but eight years in I'd be lying if I said our sex life was all that exciting. But despite all that, I did miss Jason and we got into a habit of meeting up for drinks every week or so.

Now, five years on, we're best friends and I couldn't imagine my life without him in it. We've even been on holiday together (albeit with twin beds) and had a much better time than we did when we were together. But there are times when I look at him and can't believe I ever spent most of my youth with him. There's no spark, he's got a bit of a beer gut and, lovely as he is, we're very different people. When I look back over the amount of time I spent crying over him, I can't understand why it was such a big deal. Maybe we were only ever meant to be friends.

Great ex-pectations

There are certain things that people expect of a partner that they'd never expect of a friend: rubbing your stomach when you have period pain, coming with you when you go to see your parents or telling you that you look fantastic when you're wearing a dress that any true friend would point out makes you look like a lump, to name just a few. However, it can be hard to establish where that line is with an ex who becomes a friend. After all, they used to have to abide by the stricter 'lover' rules (and get the requisite perks). You both need to recognise that things have changed. So what's acceptable to expect from an ex that you're friends with? And what's likely to send them screaming for the hills (if they're remotely sane)?

An ex who's a friend should be expected to...

- Tell you the truth.
- Treat you with respect.

- Listen.
- Help you get home safely when you go out together.
- Remember your birthday (given enough not too subtle reminders).
- Give you a hug when you really need it.

An ex who's a friend shouldn't be expected to...

- Give you all the gory details about their sex life.
- Choose who they date based on your advice.
- Answer the phone to you no matter what time of day or night it is.
- Be your automatic 'plus one' at any event you go to.
- Put your needs before their own.
- Put out.

If you find yourself feeling sad or resentful every time you see your ex, chances are your expectations and theirs don't match up. You have two options should this happen – be honest about the way you feel with a no-holds-barred chat, or walk away. Life's too short to waste time on feeling lousy.

Sex with an ex

Friendship's all well and good, but then there's the slightly murkier question of whether you should have sex with an ex? The sensible and obvious answer is a great big no, but it's not always as clear-cut as that. If you're not in love with your ex – and vice versa – it can be a way to scratch an itch without adding to the numbers or exposing yourself to more sexual health risks. Sex with an ex can sometimes act as catharsis, restoring your ego and leaving you in a fit state to walk away. And some people get a sense of relief when they have sex with an ex and realise that, once those rose-tinted glasses are off, the shagging isn't actually as good as they remembered it being.

Be warned though: if you've spent an age getting over an ex and then you bump into him and end up getting it on, you could just be setting yourself right back at the beginning. Again, this is thanks to wonder-drug oxytocin (really, if it wasn't naturally produced by the body, the authorities would ban it). The last thing you want is to feel bonded to someone you've gone through hell getting over – and your friends will be a lot less sympathetic second-time round – so think very carefully before shagging an ex that you're still emotionally involved with in any way at all.

One solution is to shag is the ex before last. So, if you split up with your partner, rather than thinking about leaping into bed with him, consider the person you split up with before that. Chances are you'll have more emotional distance from *that* ex so you'll be able to have sex with less risk of trauma (assuming they weren't the one that broke your heart interminably, and they haven't been wistfully hoping you'll get back together with them since the day you split up).

The other thing to remember about sex with an ex is that it's innately emotionally empty. It's not going to lead to a relationship so is purely about enjoying the moment. If that's what you're after then it's cool and groovy. But if you think that making the beast with two backs with an ex is a way to get them back, don't do it. You're clearly not ready for it and it'll only lead to tears. Move onto someone new instead. Or hell, masturbate. At least you know you're not going to break your own heart. Well, not unless you're very masochistic.

Avoiding ex-sex mistakes

If you're still into your ex then falling into bed with them can be all too easy a mistake to make. You need to be on your guard to make sure that you don't let yourself slip. As such, it's important that you never get drunk with an ex that you think it'd be a bad idea to make out with. Indeed, don't even go somewhere that sells alcohol with them. It's often the case that people end up getting into a much higher state of inebriation than usual when they're out with an ex because emotions can run high, and a lot of people end up drinking faster than they usually would in order to cope with feeling uncomfortable (no, this isn't a recommended course of action – it's just something that tends to happen.) Alcohol plus emotionally damaged/damaging exes is a sure-fire way to get yourself right back at the beginning of the dealing with break-up stages.

The 'Should you have sex with your ex?' checklist

Read through the list below. If you can honestly answer a definite 'no' to every single one of them then you should be able to get through sex with your ex without it leading to too much heartbreak. But don't blame me if it all goes wrong...

- I still want to get back together with my ex.
- Having sex with my ex will make him fall in love with me again.
- My ex is still in love with me.
- I dream about my ex on a regular basis.
- I get jealous thinking about my ex with another woman.
- If I shag my ex, I'll feel guilty about dating anyone else.
- My ex was physically dangerous but I still fancy him.
- My ex is with a new partner.
- I would happily have sex with my ex without a condom.
- Sex with my ex is the best I'm ever going to have in my life.
- I'm with a new partner but I still fancy my ex.

Sarah's story: Sex with my ex got me over him

When I met Phil it was love at first sight. We had a whirlwind relationship and I really thought he was 'the one', so when it ended a mere two months later, I was heartbroken. He was the best lover I'd ever had and I couldn't imagine having sex that good ever again. I sobbed over him, and yet still often thought about him late at night during 'alone time'.

It was even worse when he started seeing a big-breasted 18-year-old – almost half his age. I felt like he was saying I was past it and he wanted someone more attractive than me. I spent far too many nights crying over him and became convinced I'd never get over him

Then I bumped into him one night when I'd been at the pub with friends. I was on my way home, feeling a bit tipsy, and he was on the same tube as me. We got chatting and he offered to walk me home. He'd just split up with the 18-year-old so I saw my chance. I knew how to seduce him so I really went for it.

It worked perfectly. Soon he was in my bed and we were making out. Contrary to what I was expecting, it was distinctly average. After all the build-up in my head, I realised that he wasn't the ultimate lover. The reason sex had been so good was because I was so in love with him. Now, even though I still fancied him and had thought I wanted him back, it was nice enough but nothing special.

After that night I felt a lot better about things. I stopped crying over him and we even became friends – though we don't see each other that often. I don't really need to any more. Having sex with him was the best thing I could have done to get me over him. I only wish that I'd realised sooner.

From ex to sex

So if you've decided that sex with an ex is a good idea, how do you go from terse conversations to tight embraces? A lot of the time, things will just happen naturally. You'll meet up to exchange the things you've left at each other's houses, start talking about old times, find yourselves getting closer and closer and before you know it you're kissing, clothes are flying off and you're getting down and dirty on the floor.

Alternatively, you may go out for a drink to get 'closure' and find, three drinks down the line, that your relationship may be closed but your legs are, for some reason, open. And hell, there's nothing wrong with that if you've already made sure that he's an ex you can cope with shagging (and vice versa). Do remember that drink can affect your better judgement though, so give the 'Should you have sex with your ex' list above a little extra thought before you end up in the bedroom. That way you'll be sure you're not being led into making a mistake by the booze.

Similarly, sex with an ex often happens courtesy of 'drunken dialling' – when you go out with your friends, feel a bit frisky at the end of the night and decide to call or text your ex to help sate the urge. Again, make sure it's the right kind of ex before you do this. To help prevent yourself making drunken mistakes, it's worth deleting the number of every ex that you wouldn't have sex with from your mobile phone. Store the numbers of any exes who are now friends and would be a mistake to shag with the words 'Do not call' before their name, to give yourself a sobering reminder. And be wary of getting into the habit of making booty calls too – it's all too easy to get sucked into a lifestyle of casual sex with exes, and that can make it harder for you to move on to finding someone new.

Of course, not everyone drinks to excess, and fate doesn't always give you a helping hand. If you want to get it on with an ex and you haven't yet managed to 'accidentally' find it happening, you can manipulate a situation that'll encourage the result you're looking for. Arrange to go out with your ex then ask them to walk you home at the end of the night. The old, 'Want to come in for coffee?' can work just as well on an ex as on a new man. Avoid using phrases such as, 'We need to talk,' or even, 'It'd be good to chat to you some more,' as these are programmed into a man's head as meaning, 'Scary, must run away, she wants to discuss relationships/what went wrong'. Instead, go with a flirtatious look and maybe a cheeky grope of his bum or peck on the lips to indicate what's on offer. Throwing in a line about running out of batteries since the pair of you split up is another good – if brazen – way to tell him what you want.

Alternatively, call up your ex and tell him what you're thinking. It's important that you make it clear exactly what you're after – namely, sex – rather than a returning to any sort of a relationship. Your ex may be understandably nervous about getting into a complicated situation so you need to deal with his fears before he even has time to think about them.

No matter what approach you go for, don't sulk if your ex turns you down. Not everyone is able to have sex with an ex, and it could be that you're the only one who's looking back on your old rumpo sessions fondly. That doesn't mean you were rubbish in bed – your ex may just want to move on from the old relationship without any ties to you, which is his choice to make. Instead, bat away the embarrassment with an, 'Ah well, you can't blame a girl for trying,' and make your escape at speed.

Regardless of how it is you end up getting intimate, if you *do* have sex with an ex, it's worth employing a few tricks to stop yourself from getting too emotionally involved. Unless it can't be avoided, don't stay over with your ex after you've had sex. Casual affection such as hugging while sharing a bed, or snuggling up and drifting off to sleep together can be easily misinterpreted by one or both of you. Go for an 'afternoon delight' session instead – it has the added bonus of feeling particularly salacious to be getting intimate when you think that everyone else in the world is at work, shopping or doing their chores.

It should be obvious, but if you're shagging an ex, don't go out on romantic dates – or at least certainly not to places you went together when you were still boyfriend and girlfriend. Behave in the way that you would with a friend except for when you're doing the deed and you'll be more likely to keep your emotions – and your ex's – in check. Don't, on the other hand, feel afraid to experiment with your ex sexually. Just because you always did things one way when you were together, it doesn't mean you can't change things. After all, you're in a different type of relationship with him now, so you can be as wild (or vanilla) as you want.

Sandi's story: Exes keep me sated

When I'm dating someone I'm monogamous but in between partners, I'll shamelessly take advantage of my exes, or at least the ones that were good in bed. I'm still friends with most of them, we know what each other likes and doesn't like in bed and it doesn't feel as risky as going out and having one-night stands with strangers. I always make sure that I've got more than one on the go at the same time though. I learned that from a mistake I made years ago, when I was casually seeing one of my exes and found myself getting emotionally involved again – it was so embarrassing when he said that he'd thought we were just having fun. Now, juggling the exes means that I can keep a distance and just enjoy it for what it is: good, dirty fun with someone who already knows my body and isn't going to get all demanding on me. Sure, I'd like a boyfriend, but I don't see anything wrong with using the old ones until someone better comes along.

The pros and cons of sex with an ex

Pros

- You already know what to expect, sex-style and size-wise.
- You don't have to go out on the pull to secure a shag.
- You're not adding to the numbers or (probably) increasing your risk of catching an STI, unless he's been on a rampant unsafe sex rampage in the meantime (and if he has, what the hell are you doing even thinking about shagging him?).
- You know each other well enough to ask for what you want.
- You've already got his number, so pulling him can be as easy as merely giving him a call.

Cons

- You already know what to expect, sex-style and size-wise.
- It can make it harder for you to let go of your ex or vice versa.
- When your ex gets a new partner, it can feel like a double rejection.
- When you meet a new guy, you might feel guilty about getting it on with him.
- You might feel jealous if he has similar 'sex with an ex' agreements with other exes.

The in-betweeners

And then there are those ex relationships that fall somewhere between friendship and 'friend with benefit-ship'. The exes that linger for some other reason entirely. Here are a few of the more common types:

The business contact

You split up, he bores you rigid, you don't fancy him, but he has a wealth of business contacts that are handy for you and so you keep things amicable out of self-interest. This is fair enough in today's vicious business world, but only if he's not still in love with you. Staying in contact with someone who's going to suffer as a result of it, even (particularly) if it's in the form of slowly dying inside, is *Dynasty*-level cruel. And *Dynasty* went out of fashion 20 years ago.

Zoe's story: He still helps me out

Joe was a bit of a mistake. I met him at a networking party and we spent the whole night talking about work. I thought that the easy conversation meant we'd be good together and took him home with me that night. We had sex and before I knew it, we'd also fallen into a relationship. I realised a few weeks in that unless we were talking about work, we had nothing to say to each other, so I ended it. The problem is, he's fairly senior in marketing (I'm a PR) so he's a handy contact.

I made a point of keeping things amicable, saying I was only splitting up with him because I wasn't over my ex, so that I could still use him as a work contact. Does that make me a bad person?

The 'What did I see in him?'

You bump into him on occasion, possibly due to a shared social group. He brays with laughter, spraying half-masticated crisps over your best mate without apologising. He makes offensive jokes with punchlines that contain every 'ism' going. He has BO, bad breath and scurf over his shoulders. Or he's just plain boring. When you first met him, some pheromonal glitch meant that you were convinced he was 'the one' but now the oxytocin has worn off you just want to hang your head in shame at the thought that you ever considered him eligible. Ah well, look on the bright side – at least you didn't marry him.

Polly's story: Ashamed of my teenage past

When I look back on most of my exes, my overwhelming feeling is, 'What was I thinking?' There was the musician that turned out to be a drug dealer (who couldn't keep it up), the guy who pretended he was 25 and turned out to be 21 and was still living with his mum, the one who started off fit and put on two stone in the three months we went out together, the closet case and even one guy who seriously asked me if I'd be up for having a three-way with him and my sister. I think my man radar is seriously broken, though I never realise it until it's too late. At the moment I'm taking a break from men altogether – there don't seem to be any decent ones out there.

The 'Desperate times call for desperate measures'

This man would never get onto your 'sex with an ex' list. He wasn't that great in the sack, didn't hold that much physical appeal for you and was about as entertaining as a working men's club comedian. He wasn't as odious as the 'What did I see in him?' – there just wasn't a spark. But for some reason, if he texts or calls you when you have PMT, are feeling lonely or have just been dumped, you find yourself inviting him into your boudoir quicker than you can say 'desperate'. Chances are, once you've had your wicked way with him and your ego is restored, you'll be equally desperate – to get him out of the house. He, on the other hand, won't believe his luck so there's a strong chance he'll plague you with calls, hoping to get another invitation. And if he catches you when you're feeling low, it'll probably work, too. Have some self-esteem, girl, and don't go there. You know you'll regret it.

Lydia's story: I use him – and regret it

James really isn't my type. He's short (I like tall men), posh (I like middle-class boys) and obsessed by reading and theatre (I prefer sporty types). I only went out with him because a friend set us up and I was at a low ebb. We split up after a couple of weeks but he still calls me and somehow I always end up going out with him. I don't know why – I always swear it'll be the last time then do it again and remember why I always swear it'll be the last time within seconds of turning up. Somehow, after a couple of glasses of wine, he's less of a turn-off and when he asks me back to his, I go. I can't understand why I bother. My friends say I must secretly fancy him but I know that's not true.

The guilt tripper

Even worse than the 'Desperate times…' guy is the guilt tripper. Regardless of which one of you instigated the split (though, in all likelihood, it was you) he'll persist in calling you, emailing you and maybe even turning up at your house long after you've split up, asking you to go out 'as friends' for 'old times' sake'. If you get on with him then that's fair enough – but generally speaking, Mr Guilt Tripper is someone that you no longer want in your life. Unfortunately, he tends to turn up accompanied with a tale of woe – he's been ill, he's just been dumped, he's lost his job – so you don't feel like you can tell him where to go. Evasive action is your best bet here. Ignore his calls, block his emails and only open your front door if you're expecting company or a delivery. With any luck, he'll go away. If not, you need to front up to him and tell him that he isn't someone you want in your life. If he was, you'd have stayed together. Then thrust a box of Kleenex at him and run for the hills.

Karla's story: He gets so lonely

After I split up with Kev, I got all the friends. I'm sociable and he's not so he didn't bother to stay in contact with anyone. But it means he has no-one to go out with so when he phones up and asks me out, I feel like I have to go. I always manage to keep things friendly rather than getting off with him but in all honesty, I'd like to just stop seeing him altogether. There's nothing there between us. I just feel so guilty at leaving him on his own.

The psycho

And then there's the man who makes your life hell because you dumped him. Most of the time, this will amount to little more than surly looks or random malicious gossip about you getting passed around. The best thing to do is act with grace and ignore it. If it starts to make you really suffer, don't be afraid to report him to the police for harassment though – they're much better at dealing with nutter exes than they used to be.

Sophia's story: He got his revenge

Some bloke wasn't very happy with me when I dumped him. I woke up the next day regretting it so went to go to his house to say I was sorry. As I was closing the door I nearly died. The little fucker had carved c**t into the wooden front door for all to see (with an arrow, I guess just in case people weren't sure what house he meant, eh?). Oh by fuck, was I livid. I don't think I have been so close to killing someone in my life.

Revenge is sweet?

As Sophia found out, not all relationships end well. It could well be that your ex didn't just break your heart, he cheese-grated it then put the shreds into a blender on maximum speed. Perhaps he ran off with your best friend. Or your mum. Or your dad. Alternatively, maybe you became a nightmarish obsessive incapable of independence and scared the hell out of him. For whatever reason, many relationships end with a certain undercurrent of tension.

In these situations, it may be tempting to think about getting revenge. Stop right there. If you're feeling that much animosity towards him you're clearly not over him – you're locked in the 'anger' stage of the 'getting over a man' cycle. If you feed the anger it'll only make things worse and there's a reasonable chance he'll respond in kind – or at least with mutual anger. You could end up in a *War of the Roses*-style battle of attrition, where you're exhausted by the effort of avenging your relationship but can't stop. And that's just no fun. Instead, work your way through all the stages of 'overness' so you can come out of the other side with a smile on your face.

That said, revenge stories can be pretty funny so here are a couple from women who got their own back on men who scorned them. Don't try this at home.

Penny's story: A good comeback

I'd been with Steve for almost six months. When we first met he'd only just split with his girlfriend who was pregnant so I was wary of getting involved with him. But he kept wheedling away at me, telling me there was no way they'd get back together and eventually I caved. We started dating but after a couple of months I noticed his friends being mean to me in my local pub. I asked him about it and he said I was being silly and that they all liked me. It carried on though and really hurt. Then one day I got a phone call from his best mate. 'What the hell are you doing dating Steve when he's still with Jenny?' What! I was shocked. He'd told everyone I was trying to get him to leave his pregnant girlfriend for me, even though he told me they'd split up. I was furious.

I planned my revenge carefully. When he next came round I enticed him into bed and we had sex. Afterwards I asked him to make me a cup of tea. When he left the room I took the condom and put it, contents upwards, in the bottom of his cigarette packet, putting all the cigarettes back in to soak up what was there. They were back in his pocket before he returned with the tea. I don't know what gave me the idea – it came to me in a flash. I just wish I'd seen the look on his face when he finished the pack and realised he'd smoked his own come.

The problem with revenge is that, if discovered, you look like an obsessive freak, and if not, you still know that you've actively gone out of your way to be mean to someone, which just isn't nice. And hell, there's always the chance that Karma could come back and bite you on the arse.

Andrew's story: She was a bunny-boiling nightmare

Carrie and I went out casually for a while – or at least that's what I thought. We were students, I never promised her monogamy and I thought we were just having some fun. When she started to get a bit too keen, I told her that things were over – I wasn't ready for commitment.

The next morning I woke up to find the words 'I love you' daubed on my door in menstrual blood. I knew it was menstrual blood because she'd left the tampon on the floor outside my door, perfectly positioned for me to stand on.

I don't know what she was hoping to achieve – I can't imagine any sane guy thinking, 'Oh well, in that case I'll take you back'. Instead, there was a lot of gossip around my hall of residence and when people asked who it was that had done the deed, I told them. It might not be very gentlemanly but hey, I was young and she was weird. The next thing I heard, she'd been dubbed 'Bloodbath' and no one in our circle was remotely prepared to date her. If she'd do that after a casual fling, what would she do if something more serious ended?

Looking back I realise that there must have been something badly wrong with her and I probably hurt her more than I realised at the time, but as far as I'm concerned, what she did was still unnecessary, not to mention a revolting thing to wake up to. Needless to say I was a lot more careful about the women I picked to date from that point forwards.

OK, it's unlikely that most people would have the low self-esteem – or dark imagination – to try something quite that nasty but it only serves to illustrate that something which seems like a good idea at the time can be a huge mistake in hindsight. So unless you really can't resist – and you're certain your revenge won't be traced back to you – go with the more sensible option of taking revenge by living well, enjoying your life and proving that 'the bastard' didn't hurt you at all. That way you'll be punishing him where it really hurts: his ego.

Ten ways to tell that you're really over an ex

1. Someone asks you how you met your ex and you have to think for a moment before remembering the details.
2. When you think about the relationship you had with your ex, you get a mild pang of nostalgia at most, rather than getting angry, horny or depressed.
3. You stop comparing every other man you meet to him.

4. You hear that your ex has met the partner of their dreams and you don't care – or you feel happy for them.

5. You don't feel any need to tell everyone you date details about your ex.

6. Your best friend stops automatically reaching for the tissues whenever your ex's name is mentioned.

7. The thought of sharing a romantic evening with your ex makes you smirk at the absurdity of it.

8. When you find an old picture of the pair of you together, it acts as nothing more than a reminder of the time you spent together.

9. If the phone rings and it's your ex, your heart doesn't flip with pleasure.

10. You stop masturbating about him.

Chapter 3

Dealing with His Exes

Once you've got over your ex, you might think that your life is magically sorted. You can stop feeling over-emotional every night, move on with your life and sooner or later, find yourself getting all loved up and effusive about someone new. Life is a thing of joy and daydreams once more. Yeah, right.

With every new relationship comes a new set of relationship issues. And unfortunately, unless you have a penchant for virgins, your new man is likely to have his share of history too, so you need to deal with everyone he's ever dated and shoved into his emotional baggage (if not, with any luck, an actual suitcase).

You may not want to talk about your man's exes (and he may be unwilling to share any information about them) but it's handy to know how your man related to previous people he's dated, both during and after he went out with them. Although people don't always behave in the same way with different partners, you may be able to spot a pattern of behaviour. If that's treating his lovers with respect and breaking up merely because the partnership didn't work, it's all well and good. But if your partner's got a history of dating 'psychos', being unfaithful or being unable to hold down a relationship for anything more than a few months then it can give you the early warning you need in order to evade any unpleasantness.

Sometimes a man will say that he's over his ex – and believe it – when actually, he'd desperately love to have her back in his life. You need to know how to spot the signs that his heart still belongs to someone else and take the appropriate course of action, which comes down to your own sense of self-esteem. Do you really want to spend your time with a man who's fixated on another woman when you could be with a man who wants you and nobody else? For the sake of your sanity, it makes sense to save yourself for a man who's emotionally available rather than settling for one who'll always make you feel 'second best'. However, just because that's the sensible thing to do, it doesn't mean that you'll always want to do it, in which case it's important to know the mechanisms that will help you cope.

And your man's exes won't necessarily just enter into your relationship on a mental level. They could play an altogether more active role in your life. He may have an ex who still thinks that she's in love with him and refuses to go away, constantly plaguing him with emotive text messages and phone calls (somehow always timed to happen just at the most awkward or intimate possible moment for you). If your other half was dumped by his ex, there's a chance that he might be so resentful about it that you'll have to deal with his vitriol towards the entire female gender (it's amazing how well some men can hide their misogyny when you first meet them). Or you might have to deal with him having an ex who still sees him as a soft touch/her 'property' and calls him up to borrow cash or pick her up if she gets stranded in the middle of town late at night (which is annoying, to say the least – if anyone's going to get pampered by your man, it should be you).

Even if your man's ex behaves perfectly and he's well and truly over her, problems can still arise, particularly if he's remained friends with her. You may find yourself comparing yourself to her – or thinking that he is – and believing that you come up short. Telling a man that you don't want him to see his ex is controlling behaviour and not to be recommended, but it's not always easy to avoid feeling jealous when he goes to see someone that you know he got jiggy with in the past. You need to set boundaries, but it can be tricky knowing what's acceptable and what are domineering 'under the thumb' demands.

Every day, and almost everywhere, couples are getting into rows because a woman feels jealous of her man's relationship with his exes (and vice versa). Sometimes this is justified – insecure men may 'play' a partner by deliberately mentioning how fantastic their ex was, or being secretive about seeing their exes which can lead to paranoia. In other cases, it's down to a woman's own insecurities, in which case the only person who can solve it is her. So before you can start to tackle any issues associated with your man's exes, you need to divide them into 'his problem' and 'your problem'. If there are still emotional issues that need resolving with one of his exes – say, he's not over her, or she's not over him – then your man has to face it, well, like a man. But if you find yourself getting insecure at the idea of him spending any time with someone he's happened to date in the past, it's your own insecurity that you need to confront.

Almost every relationship problem comes down to insecurity in some way, whether it's yours, your partners or even mutual. The main problem with this is that if it's not faced head-on, you end up responding to your partner with your insecurity rather than your real personality. Here are four different versions of the same conversation to illustrate:

When he's insecure about your ex

Him: You know, I really like being with you.

You: I really like being with you too.

Him: Well, from everything you've said I've got to be better than [puts on silly voice] 'Jamie'.

You: [Defensively] Jamie wasn't that bad.

Him: So you'd rather be with him rather than me. Well, if that's what you want, maybe we should split up?

You: What the fuck?

When you're insecure about his ex

Him: You know, I really like being with you.

You: You're just saying that. I mean, your ex was five

years younger than me and the size of a twig.

Him: No, I really mean it. You're much better than her in so many ways.

You: [Defensively] You mean there are other ways that she was better than me?

Him: That's not what I said.

You: Yeah, but it's what you didn't say that matters.

Him: What the fuck?

When you're both insecure about each other's exes

Him: You know, I really like being with you.

You: I've heard that before, from Jamie. Anyway, I bet you said the same thing to Alice.

Him: When will you stop comparing me to Jamie? And why do you have to drag Alice into this?

You: [Defensively] I only made a passing comment. You're the one that kept her in the conversation. You just like saying her name, don't you? [puts on silly voice] 'Oh, Alice, I love you Alice, you're so sexy, Alice…'

Him: [Angrily talking over you] Not as bad as you and [puts on silly voice] 'God, Jamie. Oooh, Jamie, just there, Jamie, harder Jamie'.

The neighbours: What the fuck?

When you're both feeling secure

Him: You know, I really like being with you.

You: I really like being with you too.

Both: Hug and kiss.

As you can see, it's much better to have a mutually secure relationship for the sake of your own (and your neighbours') sanity. So first of all, make sure that you identify and deal with any of your own insecurities.

Your problems

One of the biggest and most common insecure issues is feeling jealous of your man's history. It's perfectly acceptable to get a vague picture of his past. However, if you spend all the time that you get with your man quizzing him about his exes in a jealous and obsessive way, you'll soon end up joining their ranks. Behaving in a jealous fashion towards a man is one of the easiest ways to make him cheat. Given enough accusations of infidelity, most men (and women) will eventually either end a relationship or think, 'If you're going to accuse me of cheating all the time, I may as well do it,' and get it on with someone else. After all, he's going to get grief from you either way, so what's the point of him remaining faithful?

Caitlin's story: She banned me from his life

I went out with Mike for a few months a couple of years ago but it didn't work out because both of us were way too similar – manic, work-obsessed and very short of time. We got on brilliantly and the sex was incredible but we knew that if we carried on seeing each other, one of us would wind up getting resentful because we hardly ever got to see each other. We stayed good friends though, and hung out whenever we got the chance, sometimes spending the night together for old time's sake. Then he met Lizzy, a pretty girl who blew him away. They started dating and he and I continued to see each other as mates, but without any rude behaviour because he was attached. I met Lizzy, we got on (at least from my point of view) and all was well.

Then she found some semi-clad pictures I'd sent him after we broke up but before he told me that he was dating her. They were only sent as a bit of a laugh, and for some reason (yes, OK, maybe I can guess why) he'd kept them. She went ballistic and banned him from seeing me ever again. He didn't like that at all and ended up dumping her. I feel a bit guilty but I can understand why he responded in the way that he did. I hadn't meant anything bad by sending the pictures and she was the one who overreacted, after all.

Even if your man's not the cheating type (no, you can't do a DNA test to find out) jealous behaviour will be a major turn-off. While it is an understandable emotion, it's also highly undesirable and ultimately self-destructive. But how do you deal with it if you're naturally a jealous person?

If you don't tend to get jealous in relationships and suddenly find yourself quizzing your man about his every move, there are a number of possible causes.

To start with, you need to get to the bottom of why it is that you feel so jealous. It could be that you've fallen in love for the first time and the intensity of the emotions is bringing your inner demons to the fore. Perhaps you were hurt by your last partner cheating on you and are assuming that all men are the same. Or maybe your man is deliberately encouraging you to feel jealous because he's insecure and needs the validation. The first two are your problems to deal with. The latter case is his problem, and will be dealt with later.

If it turns out that you're the one with the problem, look at your relationship history. Have you behaved in a jealous fashion towards every partner you've ever dated? If so, it suggests that you've got some sort of relationship issues going on that you need to confront. Perhaps your parents split up because of infidelity? Maybe you've always felt 'second best' and, as such, can't understand why someone would go out with you? You may fear that you're not sexually adventurous, attractive, interesting or intelligent enough to attract a good partner. All of these feelings are very common but until you resolve them and get a balanced view of yourself, it's unlikely you'll be able to have a fulfilling and healthy relationship with anyone else, because your relationship with yourself is so flawed.

Reprogramming yourself to get rid of any negative patterns you've learned as a child can be incredibly complex, so if you suspect your jealousy has its roots in your earliest experiences then it's well worth seeing a counsellor to help you through it. Nowadays there's no stigma attached to seeking help, and the financial cost is more than balanced out by the emotional gains to be had. The sooner you deal with the problem, the less ingrained it will be, so tackle it as soon as you become aware of it. If therapy raises issues you're not ready to deal with then you can always stop treatment and go back to it once you've had time to process things on your own.

Some things that may help you cope with negative patterns learned through your childhood include:

- *Talking to your parents — ideally both of them — about what happened.* Your perspective could be very different from theirs, and it may well be that their explanation of events helps you move on. For example, you might believe that your father cheated on your mother because 'all men are bastards' — possibly from over-hearing your mum chatting to her mates about it at the time. With the benefit of hindsight, and a bit of distance from events, your mum may admit that the relationship had been faltering for a while, that she'd cheated on him first or even that she'd pushed him towards cheating because she didn't want to be in the relationship but was scared of dumping him. You can never know the real story behind a relationship break-down, and a child's perspective on events is often skewed (just look at the amount of kids out there who believe their parents splitting up was all their fault). As such, discovering the 'adult' explanation may help you get a new and healthier perspective on events, and stop you from continuing the pattern into your own adult life.

- *Writing down a list of situations that make you feel jealous.* It could be that you spot a pattern and can then focus on getting to the root of that. For example, if you always tend to get jealous when you're out with your partner at a party and everyone is glammed up, this could be because you always felt like you were badly dressed as a teenager and everyone was judging you negatively on your appearance. As such, being with other people looking 'better than you' can bring up lurking insecurities.

- *Therapy.* However, not all problems stem from your childhood. If you don't think that you learned any negative patterns as a kid yet you still find yourself feeling jealous in a relationship, it's worth examining your sense of self-worth. Nowadays the media presents an image of 'superwoman', in which women are expected to be slim, attractive, successful in business and sexually voracious and adventurous. Obviously, this is utterly unattainable and yet the constant bombardment with images of women who are apparently 'living the dream' can make it feel like you're the only one who doesn't match up. You may even feel that you have friends who are managing to juggle the myriad things modern women are expected to with ease but this is only because they're good at faking it, guaranteed. Underneath the façade they'll be feeling just as insecure about one or more aspects of themselves. Just ask them if you don't believe me.

Rather than judging yourself by other people, you need to judge yourself by your own standards. After all, you never really know what another person's life is like – you can only see what they choose to show you. By comparison, you know exactly what's going on in your own life – and if any part of it isn't up to scratch, you can sort it.

Let's say that you don't feel attractive. Time and time again surveys come out showing that confidence has at least as much bearing on how attractive other people perceive you to be as your actual physical attributes. As such, focus on making yourself feel good and you'll look good. Sure, you may choose to give yourself a make-over to assist in the feeling good stakes, but what's on the outside is way less important than what's on the inside.

To boost your confidence, write a list of all the things that are good about you – maybe you're great at UNIX or cook the best roast dinner ever; perhaps you've got an infectious giggle, or are a good listener. There's a lot more to being attractive than having a good body and pretty face, and a great personality really will reap you more rewards in the long term. So remind yourself about all of your positive traits and you'll seem much hotter to other people.

If your problem is feeling that you're not sexually adventurous enough, or are lacking in skill, get some books and read up on tips and techniques. You don't need to swing from the chandeliers to be a good lover. Neither should you feel obliged to follow 'sex trends' – just because the magazines say that swinging is 'in' or 'every-one is trying bondage', it doesn't mean that it's right for you. Real sexual confidence is about doing what you want, when you want, with the person that you want to do it with, and feeling unashamed to ask for what you want (or say no to what you don't want). Taking a 'tick-box' approach to sex where you assume that you have to experiment wildly to be a good lover is not the route to sexual nirvana. Instead, masturbate regularly so that you know what turns you on, communicate with your partner and don't be afraid to fantasise, and you'll be perfectly adventurous enough to have great sex.

Maybe your intelligence is the thing that you're insecure about? If so, remember that no-one can know everything and the most intelligent people are those who realise that they still have a lot to learn. So what if your boyfriend's ex could speak 17 languages? Chances are that you've got better social skills or you've read more books or you've got a more encyclopedic knowledge of music than she has. More to the point, another person's strength is not your weakness. Focus on what you do know about and relax about what you don't. Should a man (or indeed, woman) makes snide comments about your intelligence, it suggests they're more flawed than you are because their insecurity makes them have to label themselves as 'bright' and reinforce that label by belittling other people. If you're really worried, you can always go and learn more – education doesn't have to stop when you leave school.

And if you fret that you're not as interesting as other people, relax. Everyone feels that way at some stage. Research has found that people who listen – and nothing else – are considered to be the most interesting people in the room so if all else fails, keep your mouth shut and your ears open and you'll be deemed a sparkling conversationalist.

There's also a chance that you might be jealous because a previous partner cheated on you. If so, it's highly unfair to take it out on your new man. One bad apple doesn't mean you should give up eating them for life.

By dealing with your own insecurities, you should find that your jealousy lessens and eventually melts away. All too often jealousy comes from a fear of losing someone because you don't deem yourself to be good enough, so once you realise that you are — hell, anyone should be grateful to be with you — then you'll turn into much better relationship material, and feel happier in yourself too. That kind of result has got to be worth a bit of self-analysis, hasn't it?

The amateur detective

If you don't deal with your jealousy, you could find your-self committing the unforgivable act of snooping around your man's house, trying to find evidence of his exes, or worse. If any of the below sound remotely familiar (in increasing levels of badness) stop doing them right now.

You're heading for psycho-land if...

- Your man mentions his ex's name and you Google her as soon as you get home (or worse, check her out by Blackberry, from the pub).
- You forage through his drawers to see if he has anything left in them that belonged to her — and throw out anything that you find so that he doesn't have any reminders of the past.

- You read your man's email and check his instant messaging log when he's not around.
- You 'accidentally' flick through your man's phone numbers/text messages when he leaves his mobile phone on the table.
- You call her to quiz her about exactly what happened between them.
- You turn up at her place of work and follow her home to check that she's not seeing him.
- You break into her flat.

Even if you do learn something about your man's ex by spying on him or snooping around, you won't be able to do anything about it without admitting to your man that you got all obsessive and scary, so you may as well save yourself the time and bother. Added to which, chances are that anything you find won't be conclusive – it will only fuel further questions in your mind since what you really want to know is exactly how your man really feels about his ex and the only person who can give you a real and honest answer about that is the man himself. The more you snoop in vain hope of getting clues, the more likely you are to find a red herring (say, a bottle of perfume in his bathroom that his sister left there the last time she stayed), and the more curious you're going to feel. Even *not* finding any evidence of impropriety may lead you to feeling that he must have hidden his past particularly carefully, suggesting that he's got something to be ashamed of.

What it boils down to is that spying on your man will only hurt yourself. More to the point, if you're so insecure that you can't trust your man to tell you anything important about his exes, and so lacking in communication skills that you can't ask him about anything that worries you, chances are you're not in a good place to have a relationship anyway.

Ruth's story: I helped him move house to discover his past

Jack moved house a month after we got together. He was complaining about what a pain it would be so I offered to help. He accepted saying that I was 'an angel', but, if I'm being honest, I wanted to find out more about his life and helping him move gave me the perfect opportunity.

I started off in the kitchen so he wouldn't suspect anything – who keeps personal stuff in their kitchen, after all? Being female, I was much faster than him at organising things though, and before long I was done so he said I could move to the lounge.

In there, I headed straight for his desk. The top drawer was full of photos. I 'accidentally' dropped them (quietly) on the floor, giving me a chance to snoop. There he was with his ex (I assume it was her anyway, as there were hundreds of pictures of them on holiday, with his arm round her and even one of them in bed together, clearly taken by him stretching his arm out). She was prettier than he'd described her and I felt sick as I looked at them cosily together. That triggered something in me. Bundling the pictures into a box, I started looking through the rest of the drawers for letters, ticket stubs – anything that could tell me more about their relationship. The second drawer was full of business stuff but in the third drawer down, I hit the jackpot: it was crammed with letters from her, all saying how much she loved him and how he was the best lover ever – in graphic detail. I wanted to stop reading but my eyes were glued to the page. My eyes welled up and it was only when a tear rolled out and splashed onto the paper, smearing the ink, that I realised how badly I was behaving. I hurriedly shoved the letters back into another box and set about packing his computer instead.

That night, I couldn't forget what she'd written. When Jack touched me, I froze, remembering her words about his fingers on her skin. I pretended I'd got a headache but I know he felt me recoil.

From that day onwards, I was paranoid. Her words wouldn't leave my head and I couldn't tell Jack what I'd done – I knew he'd hate me for invading his privacy. We split up a few weeks later because, in his words, I wasn't being myself. I sometimes wonder what would have happened if I hadn't been so nosy and I'd just carried on getting to know him in a normal way.

Ex-emplary behaviour

Although it might seem like a lot to cope with, most of the major ex dilemmas will probably be dealt with fairly early on in your relationship. You'll spot the warning signs, bail out if it's too much for you to deal with and resolve anything that's just a minor problem. However, there are ongoing issues that may crop up, particularly if your man is friends with any of his exes. You could find your jealousy strings getting pulled on and feel a need to ask questions and set boundaries.

You do need to be careful about what questions you ask your partner. While a certain amount of digging is entirely acceptable, you don't automatically get the right to know everything about a man's relationship history the second you start dating him. He's got as much of a right to privacy about his past as you have.

Good questions to ask your new partner

- Have you got or have you ever had an STI?
- How long ago did you split up with your ex?
- Why did you split up?
- Were you in love or was it just a casual thing?
- How do you feel about your ex now?

Bad questions to ask your new partner

- Am I better looking than your ex?
- Am I the best in bed out of everyone you've ever dated?
- What was your ex's top turn-on?
- What was the worst thing your ex did in bed?

Obviously, there are also acceptable and unacceptable things to demand from your man. Every relationship should have boundaries and you need to make sure that you're not letting yours become obsessive and hard to deal with.

Bunny-boiler demands
I insist that you…

- Delete your exes numbers from your phone.
- Get rid of every picture you have of any exes.
- Stop seeing any friends who know your ex.
- Delete all your exes from your instant messaging account.
- Stop crashing over with exes who are now friends, after a night out.

Sane woman requests
Darling, will you…

- Delete the number of the ex who keeps on calling and saying she loves you.
- Get rid of all the naked pictures you have of any exes.
- Let me know if you're going to a social event that your ex might be at.
- Stop talking to any exes that send you naked pics over instant messenger.
- Stop sharing a bed with your ex.

As a general rule, don't ask your man to do anything that you'd find unacceptable for him to demand of you. And don't ask anything about his ex that you'd find unacceptable for an ex's new partner to ask about you. Similarly, don't request any information from your partner about his exes that you wouldn't be comfortable sharing with him about your exes. Try to empathise with your partner and, no matter how curious you are, only ask what you think are acceptable questions that you're certain you can cope with having him answer honestly.

If your man stays friends with his ex then the need for boundaries becomes even more important. Let's say your man goes out with his ex on a regular basis. That's fair enough as long as he doesn't cancel on you to go and see her, or prioritise her above you in any other way. However, there's nothing wrong with asking if you can meet your man's ex, particularly if he spends a significant amount of time with her. Don't insist on meeting her before you 'allow' him to see her. However, once you've been dating for a while and he's met her three or more times over the course of your relationship, it's entirely acceptable to say that you'd like to be introduced to her.

If your boyfriend's been mates with his ex for a while, and was single for that time, he may have got into the habit of sharing a bed with her non-sexually after a night out. This is something that you're well within your rights to ask him not to do any more (it may sound obvious but you'd be surprised how many people get into rows about this one). Even if it is perfectly innocent, there's an intimacy to sharing a bed with someone that can feel understandably threatening. Added to this, when a man and a woman share a bed, it's fairly usual for 'something to come up' if they cuddle, even if neither has any intention of taking things further. Your man's erection is not something that should be pressed against another woman (unless you're in an open relationship). You're not being a possessive nightmare by asking him to keep his stiffies for you (and himself) alone.

And then there's the less obvious stuff: souvenirs of past relationships. While it's overly controlling to ask a man to get rid of anything he's ever been given by another woman, to destroy all pictures and to never speak of the past again, you shouldn't be expected to put up with him having photos of her all over the house. Any mementos should be locked in a box so that they're memories rather than constant reminders. Don't even think about raising the issue until you've been with each other for at least a month, and have already had the 'are we boyfriend and girlfriend?' discussion though – otherwise you'll look way too keen and, frankly, scary.

It might all sound like common sense but it's amazing how quickly all that can fly out the window once all the loved-up chemicals kick in. By keeping an eye on your behaviour you can make sure that you don't inadvertently turn into a psycho and end up accumulating another ex for your collection. Then all you need to do is make sure that you both deal with his issues in a mature and balanced fashion...

His problems

Yes, there are numerous ex-factors that fall squarely into being 'his problem'. In most cases, these are because your man needs to do some baggage reclaim of his own, or at the very least admit that he has a problem (always easier said than done given men often don't like to show their weaknesses). While you can help your partner with his problems, he needs to be prepared to face up to them. If not, you might be able to gloss over the cracks but it'll only work as a temporary veneer.

He's still hung-up on his ex

When it comes to exes, the number-one male issue is still being obsessed by the last woman that broke his heart, months or even years after the relationship ended. Sometimes this is easy to spot and at other times it won't surface until things start to get serious between you both, and he realises that he might be exposing himself to getting hurt again. Once you spot this behaviour there's only one real solution. Two words: dump him. What do you mean you're prepared to put up with endless comparisons to another woman, strange moments of silence and a general feeling of being second-best? Where's your self-esteem?

Sometimes it's easy to gauge if your man's a love liability. Obviously, if he has pictures of his ex up on the wall (or worse, next to the bed) and gets a mournful 'what if?' look on his face whenever her name is mentioned, he's not over her. You can establish this in the first few dates and avoid getting emotionally involved with him. He might be fine for a bit of frivolous fun but anything more than a casual affair is only going to lead to getting hurt.

Another more subtle sign that he's damaged goods, and no use to any woman in a relationship until he sorts himself out, is if he constantly complains about what a nightmare his ex is. It might feel good when he tells you that you're so much better than she was because you actually move when you're having sex, or can conduct a conversation using words comprising more than two syllables, but even negative comments are a sign that he's still thinking about her. Chances are he's still in the 'anger' stage of the grieving process and, as such, has a long way to go before he's 'cured'. Again, it's easy enough to spot this behaviour early on in a relationship, and it's best to give this man a wide berth.

If your man is just out of a long-term relationship, it's even more likely he won't be over his ex. Although there may well be rebound tales with happy endings, I've certainly never heard one. No matter how convinced he is that he doesn't want to get back together with his ex, there's likely to be enough damage done to make him no good to any woman. Be friends with a man who's newly single; have sex with a man who's newly single; but whatever you do, avoid having a relationship with a man who's newly single.

If it's too late and you've already fallen into a relationship with a man who's only just out of a long-term relationship, or is hung-up on his ex, prepare yourself for comparisons, both positive and negative. Don't be surprised if his sexual techniques follow the same pattern every time – it's the one that she taught him and you'll need to invest time in reminding him that his ex was just one woman, and that every woman is different. There's a strong chance that emotional baggage will surface along the way too; either he'll suddenly realise that he's not actually emotionally ready to have a relationship even though he thought that he was, he'll decide that he wants to play the field or he'll turn into a misery guts, taking all the resentments he has towards his ex-girlfriend out on you.

If your man still clearly has issues loitering around the place from his ex-girlfriend, the best way for him to deal with them is by talking to her. You can't provide any answers whereas she can. Yes, there's the risk that he'll get back together with her if they meet up, but the risk of you breaking up if he doesn't deal with the issues is just as strong, if not stronger. So be the grown-up and encourage him to face his demons.

Then there's the trickier problem of when your man seems to be perfectly over his ex and only starts to show signs of pining a few months into the relationship, once you become settled (and quite possibly in love). Now you're in a tricky situation. You won't necessarily feel that you can just drop him because you've got emotions as well as time invested in him. Depending on his symptoms, it can be worth hanging in there.

If he starts to mention her on occasion but in a casual, 'Oh yes, that's where Jen and I went on holiday' kind of way, it could just be that now things are getting serious, you're reminding him of the last time that he fell in love. If, on the other hand, he starts to rant about how awful his ex was, having not talked about her before, or suddenly mentions how fantastic she was (and batters your self-esteem in doing so) on a regular basis, sorry, but he's probably not going to be any use to you and you may as well move on before you get even more hurt.

Daisy's story: I loved him but he loved her

I've always sworn that men who are just out of relationships are a no-go area but I broke my vow for Chris. He'd split up from his girlfriend six months before we met. They'd only dated for two years so I thought that would be enough time for him to sort himself out. I was wrong. Just at the point when I fell in love with him, three months into the relationship, he announced that he'd suddenly realised he wasn't over her. I'd been holding out on committing to him, even though he'd been pushing the pace of things, so it was particularly galling to finally give in only for him to reject me. I think I'm going to give up on men. They're just too fucked up.

How to tell that he's not over his ex

1. His conversation is abnormally peppered with mentions of things that they did together or details of her personality.

2. He refers to her as 'the bitch' and endlessly tells you how glad he is that he's finally over her.

3. He still has photos of her up in his house.

4. He massively overreacts when you do something that he doesn't agree with.

5. He constantly compares you to her, whether positively or negatively.

6. He uses expressions such as, 'You're always like this,' when you're only a few weeks into the relationship – chances are he's blaming you for every mistake his ex made too.

7. He calls her name out during sex or suddenly uses a pet name for you and looks embarrassed when you ask him why he's chosen that particular term of endearment.

8. He goes quiet and subdued after you've shared a romantic moment together.

9. He insists on leading you past the place where she works and kissing you in front of her office to prove how 'over her' he is.

10. He still has a bathroom littered with her toiletries and a drawer full of her clothes.

If you're in love and really convinced that you want to see things through, despite all the warning signs, it's important that when he exhibits a symptom of still being in love with her, you discourage his negative behaviour. As with your own behaviour, there are certain things that it's acceptable for him to expect and other things that you're well within your rights to complain about. You have no right to stop your partner from seeing his exes, helping his exes or keeping his exes' phone numbers. But there are things that are decidedly out of order and which you really shouldn't have to put up with. Here are some of the most common demands, and how to deal with them:

He keeps a picture of her next to the bed.
Ask him to move it into a drawer. He's asking way too much if he expects you to get it on with him when his ex is looking at you from his bedside table. If he refuses, don't stay overnight at his place.

He mentions her name every other sentence.
Ignore it. He may well be doing it to get a rise out of you so if you don't pay any attention — much in the way that the best way to stop a kid having a tantrum is to pretend there's nothing unusual going on — he'll soon get bored and stop his infantile behaviour.

He compares you negatively to her.
Return the favour and start talking about your well-hung ex, your millionaire ex or your football-genius ex. Who

cares if they only exist in your imagination? That said, it's going to be a pretty dull relationship if you spend you're entire time playing ex one-upmanship games.

He bitches about her all the time.
Tell him to go to see her to sort things out. If he's got issues, he should raise them with her rather than you because there's nothing you can do to make things better.

He calls out her name during sex.
Go home if you're at his place or kick him out if he's at yours. Make him grovel. You should be able to milk this one for at least one expensive meal and a bunch of flowers.

Helping a man get over his ex

It's not just the symptoms that you need to deal with. If your partner isn't over his ex and you want to stay with him then you're going to have to help him through it. Now doesn't that sound fun? Your man may have issues letting go of the past for the following reasons:

He never found out why it was they split up so didn't get to complete his relationship narrative.
As you know, it's much easier to get over a relationship when you have a beginning, middle and end to the story — namely, a complete narrative. If your boyfriend never managed to finish that last chapter, it's no wonder he's still got the book open. In order for him to move on, he needs to get resolution for the story. By far the best way

to do this – though not necessarily the easiest – is to talk to his ex partner. Only she will be able to tell him what went wrong. Any answers given to him by other people will only elicit a, 'Maybe she was thinking that, but perhaps she was thinking *this*...' response. His ex is the only person that can give him definitive answers rather than speculation.

Encouraging your man to meet up with his ex is hardly the easiest thing in the world – for you or for him. There's a reasonable chance that you'll feel jealous or resentful, not least because she's the one standing in the way of your potentially good relationship. There's a good chance that he won't want to meet up with someone that broke his heart. And there's even a risk that, once things are resolved, they'll get back together. Sadly, you can't guarantee the outcome – but you can guarantee that it'll be very hard for him to get over her and commit fully to a relationship with you unless he does see her, so it's a bit of a no-win situation.

If your man refuses to meet up with his partner, she refuses to meet him, or you can't bring yourself to raise the topic, you have two choices. Either encourage your partner to seek counselling so he can throw out the baggage left over from his last relationship, or spend hours and hours and hours talking it through with him until even he gets bored by the subject and can finally put it to one side. Who knows, such intense conversation may even bring you closer. Or it could mash your heart and end up killing the relationship stone dead. Fun stakes when you're sorting out major emotional issues, eh?

He felt the reasons that they split up were unfair.

A sense of injustice is something else that can linger long after a relationship ends. Perhaps your man felt as if he was being judged based on a lie (say, his ex suspected he was cheating and dumped him for it when actually he'd remained totally faithful). Maybe he was a 'wronged party' because she dumped him in front of his mates. Or perhaps he thought that the entire break-up was based on both parties misunderstanding what the other person was saying.

As with an incomplete relationship narrative, the only person that can really give him answers is his ex. If she's not prepared to – or he's not prepared to see her – then it's down to him to work through his resentment. He may need to examine his own behaviour here to reach resolution: perhaps he didn't cheat on his ex but always flirted with her friends or was considering cheating when she dumped him. Maybe he'd been telling all his mates that he was going to dump her but she'd got in first. Perhaps he was lousy at communication throughout the relationship, which is the real reason that they split up. The most bitterly held resentments often come from inverted guilt – you feel outraged that someone suspected you of doing something that you were secretly considering doing – and in your mind that's just not fair. Your man needs to stop stamping his feet like a toddler, admit his part in the 'injustice' and move on. After all, he's got a lovely new girlfriend now, and she's behaving more than fairly towards him.

The Ex Factor

He treated his ex badly and is full of self-loathing now that he's outside the situation and can see what mistakes he made.

Guilt is a wonderful emotion to poison yourself with. A man who feels guilty about the way that he treated his ex may find it hard to accept that anyone else could love him, because he behaved in such an offensive way. As such, he may put up barriers to intimacy, running away the second that you start to get close to him. Alternatively, he may try overly hard to be nice, smothering you with so much affection that you feel like pushing him away. In order to get over this, your man needs to apologise to his ex and forgive himself. He doesn't have to see her – he could just write her a letter explaining how sorry he is. This shouldn't just be done to alleviate his guilt – there should be genuine remorse or it's just a manipulative thing to do. Sending a bunch of flowers probably wouldn't go amiss either, as long as his behaviour wasn't so reprehensible that the idea of keeping a gift sent by him in the house would make his ex wince. Once he's apologised, he can move on. And promise you firmly that he'll never do anything an iota as unpleasant to you.

She dumped him but has come crawling back now that he's attached because she doesn't want anyone else to have him.

This is mean and petty behaviour but sadly, it's not exactly rare. It's amazing how much more attractive a discarded man becomes once another woman has picked him up and given him a polishing.

The best way to act here is to stand back with dignity and let your man make his choice. There's no point in putting up a fight – though setting a time limit on his decision is entirely acceptable (if not essential for your self-esteem). If you try to rush the matter, he'll probably panic but if you give him a bit of space, he'll either realise that his ex is a nightmare and what she's doing is immature and pathetic, or he'll go back to her, thus proving that he's an idiot. You can do better than an idiot so let him go.

He only went out with you on the rebound and realised too late that he's not ready for a relationship.
This can be heartbreaking to discover, not least because it can take a while to surface, by which time you've got emotionally involved. It is possible to salvage a rebound relationship if you give your man enough time and space – perhaps even taking a break from dating for a while so that he has a chance to get his feelings together without any distractions. It might seem hard but you can't force someone to love you, just as you can't force them to stop loving someone else. If you're convinced that he's 'the one', all you can do is wait. Don't try to speed up his decision by convincing him how great you are or slagging off his ex. This sort of behaviour will only make you less likely to get your man. Do make sure that you go out and have fun while he's trying to figure out what's going on in his head, at the very least. Otherwise you'll only find yourself sitting at home, depressed and waiting for the phone to ring. And do give yourself a time limit on waiting. No man is worth waiting for forever.

Dealing with a damaged woman-hater

If a man's last girlfriend was so cruel to him that he's decided every woman is a bitch then it's entirely possible for him to turn into a woman-hater. Symptoms include sleeping around, refusing to use a condom, asking for deliberately demeaning sex acts, standing you up at short notice, telling his friends about what you get up to in bed, humiliating you in public and telling you that you're worthless – sometimes the whole lot. If you really want to date a man like this, you need to take a closer look at your own self-esteem – surely you can do better? If you're convinced that it's love and he's just a bit broken at the moment, prepare yourself for a rough ride. You need to develop a skin of Kevlar to bounce away all those jibes. You'll need patience (and friends who are available at short notice) to cope with the endless nights when you've been stood up, and you'll need to get rid of any hint of a jealous streak so that you can turn a blind eye to his infidelities. Christ, are you really sure you want to put yourself through all this? OK, well, while you're wearing your bulletproof armour and generally waiting him out, you need to boost his self-esteem. This can be tricky as he may hate women so much that he's not prepared to listen to overt compliments. Instead, you may have to show your man that not all women are being evil behind their seemingly thoughtful actions. Over time, they might sink in and turn him back into a normal, decent man. Either that or you may end up being a doormat. Good luck.

With any of the above, the most sensible option is actually to dump him. Otherwise you run the risk of being trapped in a one-sided relationship because, for example, he's still in love with someone else and isn't available to appreciate how fabulous you are. However, it's not always easy to do the sensible thing. But please do be careful if you try to work things through – you really are running the risk of getting horribly hurt.

What his ex-style says about him

It's not just your man's individual exes that can affect your relationship. You should also bear in mind his general relationship history. Sure, people change over time but a *pattern* of behaviour should, at the very least, give an indication of what he's like. And a pattern of *negative* behaviour should trigger warning bells so you can hold off getting emotionally invested until you've got to know him a lot better. After all, as with any kind of investment, emotional investments can go down as well as up. There are numerous ways that your man's past can have an effect on your relationship – and they're not always as obvious as you might think. Here are a few of the most common:

He's only dated 'psychos'

When a man talks about his exes, you need to bear in mind you're only getting one side of the story. He may tell you all about the nightmares he's had with clingy women who kept on calling after he'd split up with them, turned up at his house unannounced or slapped him when they saw him in public, but if every ex he's had seems to fall into this trap, it could say more about him than it does about them. Perhaps he didn't have the guts to dump them and just stopped taking their calls, so when they were 'obsessively calling' him, in reality they were just trying to find out where they stood. If every woman he's dated turned up on his doorstep unannounced, it could well be that they just wanted to get their belongings back (or cash that he borrowed off them). And if he's been slapped in public by more than one ex then it could be that he's got a history of cheating or otherwise behaving in a caddish fashion.

Of course, it could just be that he's bad at choosing women and has been unlucky. But if someone keeps on choosing partners that are bad for them, even if they haven't done anything actively wrong, it does suggest underlying insecurities that could cause conflict in your relationship too.

If every tale your man tells you about his ex seems to be full of woe, it's worth doing some digging. The best way to learn the real story is to see if you can get his ex's view of things – though you have to be careful of taking this approach as it could make you look obsessive. But if possible, see if you can find out any more information from his friends. A subtle, 'God, Mark was telling me about his ex, she sounds like a nightmare,' may be enough to open the floodgates on the real story. And if your man's story is corroborated? Just make sure that you don't act like a psycho if your relationship ends because he clearly has no qualms about telling other people nightmare stories about his love life.

Sandi's story: He made me out to be insane

When I got together with Marcus, I thought he was lovely. He was good-looking with a cheeky smile and was brilliant at rugby, which always makes me weak at the knees. He did tell me that he was going through some problems with his ex, Claudia, as she refused to let go of the relationship, but other than him occasionally having to turn his phone off at 2 am when she called, it didn't really affect me.

After a few months, things were going really well. I'd met his parents and he'd even asked me to move in with him. I thought he was 'the one'. We arranged to go out to dinner to celebrate that Friday night and I spent ages getting dressed up. When I arrived at the restaurant, he wasn't there, but he was always a bit late so I didn't panic and just ordered myself a drink. An hour later he still hadn't arrived and I was beginning to worry he'd been in an accident. I called his mobile but it kept going through to voicemail. When I still hadn't managed to raise him by midnight, I was really panicked. I had his best friend's number so I called him to find out if he'd heard from Marcus. He said that Marcus had been down the pub all night with the lads.

I was furious. I'd been sitting in a restaurant on my own for half the night, and crying over what might have happened to him for the rest of it. I kept trying Marcus and he just didn't answer the phone. I left him an angry message saying that the least he owed me was an explanation but he still didn't call back.

I thought that maybe he'd got drunk so waited for him to call me the next day but he didn't. Every time I tried to call him it went straight through to voicemail. After a week of trying my mates told me that I had to give up, but I still tried him once a week or so for the next month. I couldn't believe that things could have ended so abruptly without any warning.

In the end, I called his best mate to see if he could explain what had happened. He told me to stop calling Marcus, and that he was fed up of being the go-between. Apparently Claudia had also called this particular friend to find out why things had ended with her and Marcus too. Suddenly I saw all her 'psycho' behaviour in a different light. If he'd done the same to her as he did to me, it was no wonder she was calling him at 2 am. Men like that should come with a health warning.

He's cheated on every partner he's had

If a man comes clean that he's cheated on all his exes, or even a substantial amount of them, he does deserve a few points for honesty. After all, it doesn't exactly cast him in a good light. However, it's also a warning that you should handle him with care. Once a cheater, always a cheater — or at least, research has found that if someone's cheated before then they're more likely to again. Sometimes it's because they don't think they're good enough to hold on to any one woman, so they like to have a fallback. Sometimes it's because they grew up in a home with an unfaithful male role model so believe that it's 'normal' behaviour. And other times it's simply because they're scum that are led by their dicks.

That said, some men do realise the error of their ways and grow up. This is more likely to happen with guys as they start to get older, particularly if they've had a long-term relationship that ended through cheating then spent a long time single and realised it's not as much fun on the other side of the fence as they thought. However, if a man's reached his 40s and cheated on every lover he's ever had, you'll have to get damned lucky for him to remain faithful to you. He knows how easy it is, he's got his excuses honed and he's got a taste for it. Stay with this kind of man at your own peril – you're likely to get hurt.

When it comes to dealing with a previously unfaithful man, don't get paranoid and accuse him of cheating on you all the time – it'll only backfire. However, if he starts to behave in a suspicious manner, leaving the room when his phone goes, not letting you stay over at his house or saying, 'I thought I'd bring you here because I know it's your favourite place,' about somewhere you've never been to before, don't ignore the warning bells. Leopards may change their spots but only if they have access to peroxide.

Amanda's story: I was the only one he stayed faithful to

When I met Gary he was very honest about his past. He'd got divorced a few years back because he had an affair. He'd then moved in with his mistress but they'd split up when he cheated on her too. He said that he'd only done it because he'd picked the wrong women but it didn't give me great hopes for our relationship. Still, he was fun and I went against my better judgement to carry on seeing him.

The longer we were together, the more I heard about his exes and it soon appeared that he'd cheated one everyone he'd ever been with, except for me. If I'm honest, I felt quite smug – at least until we split up because he said I did too many little things that annoyed him. He was dating another woman within a week of us splitting up. Now I wonder if there was anything going on beforehand – we did both know her and she'd always flirted with him. I guess I'll never know, and I'd rather think that he was faithful to me, if only for the sake of my own ego. He did say that he was, after all, and he'd been honest about all the other women he'd cheated on so I don't see why he'd lie.

He's never dated anyone for more than a few months

It may seem harsh to judge someone for a lack of luck in long-term relationships, but there can often be a reason for a man to have only had relatively short-term flings (youth aside). Sometimes it's because he suffers from commitment issues – once things start to get serious he gets scared and runs away. In other cases, the guy concerned may be a perfectionist and bail out at the first sign of a flaw in their partner. Or it could be that he's lousy at picking suitable partners for himself, which is a bit of a giveaway that he has low self-esteem or an unrealistic perception of himself.

It shouldn't take you long to figure out which category your man fits into. If he cancels a date on you when you mention you're feeling a bit pre-menstrual, he probably fits into the first category (though dealing with PMT-crazed women isn't exactly fun so don't hate him too much). Should he go quiet if you mention developing feelings for him, or insist that he 'needs a lot of space' in relationships, then he's almost certainly a commitment-phobe.

If he complains about seeing you without make-up on, or gets annoyed should you exhibit any taste that's different to his then he probably falls into the second category. Trying to be perfect all the time is bloody hard work. So unless you fancy getting up at dawn to put your face on so he never sees you looking less than flawless, adopting his taste in music and generally sacrificing your personality to his, he's also worth giving a wide berth.

But if he's merely lousy at picking partners for himself, things aren't necessarily so disastrous. If you think that you're well suited, it could be that he's finally grown up and figured out what he really wants in a relationship (either that or your perception of what makes a good partner is just as skewed as his). Who knows, maybe this relationship will be the one that helps him break his one-month limit. And on the plus side, it means you get to be the first girlfriend he's had a serious relationship with, so it'll feel extra-special to both of you.

There is, of course, another option: that he wanted to sow his wild oats when he was younger but over time he's realised that he doesn't need unfulfilling encounters any more. If you manage to land a man at this stage, you've hit the jackpot: he's experienced enough to be sexually skilled, sated enough not to have a wandering eye, and free of any significant previous relationships so you don't have to panic about comparing yourself to his exes. It can take time to suss out whether a man falls into the final category, so don't be too hasty and end up making a rash decision. A converted commitment-phobe is in it for keeps – it just takes the right woman and, more importantly, the right time of life to change his attitude.

Maggie's story: I thought I was different. I was wrong

Tom and I met in a bar and ended up in bed that night (don't judge me – he's really cute and you would have leapt in to bed with him the second you got a chance to as well). The next morning he asked me out to lunch and we discovered how much we had in common. We arranged a date for a few days later and that went just as well. We'd chatted about previous boyfriends and girlfriends and I was surprised that, aged 33, the longest he'd been out with someone was for a month. He's an interesting and good-looking bloke so I couldn't see what the problem could be.

On our third date, I found out. We went to the zoo and had a lovely day together, walking round holding hands, talking as if we'd known each other for ages and, if I'm honest, from my point of view at least, falling for each other. When we left the zoo we decided to go for Sunday lunch together and found a perfect pub with a log fire. Then we went back to his, had (good) sex and lay in front of the TV together, holding hands and snuggling up. I hadn't felt so happy with a man for ages, so I was shocked when he said we 'needed to talk'. I'm old enough to know that those words never bode well.

He said that he'd had a wonderful day – almost perfect – but that he didn't feel as if he was in love with me, and if he wasn't in love after such a fantastic day then he never would be. I was gutted – his logic didn't make any sense to me. I mean, I was feeling as if I *could* fall for him, but it takes a lot more than a few good dates to actually fall in love with someone. I tried to explain that to him but he said that he believed in the thunderclap and if he hadn't felt that in the first few dates, he knew he never would. Obviously, we split up – I didn't have much choice in the matter. I still bump into him from time to time and he's still single, even though two years have passed since our dates and I've gone out with several people since. Romantic as the idea of love at first sight is, I just think he's got unrealistic expectations.

He's fallen in love with every partner he's ever had

Romantic as this may sound, a man who falls for every woman he's ever been with has probably got intimacy issues. While you may think that this is a conflict — how can you be scared of intimacy if you always fall in love? — it's easy enough to understand when you think about it. Falling in love with every person you meet means that you're actually drawn to the act of being in love rather than the person you're apparently falling for. Anyone will do as long as they help you get that 'love' feeling. Once reality surfaces and anything that doesn't fit with the idealised view of love comes to the fore, that love will die as quickly as it appeared. As such, someone who falls in love all the time is actually trying to avoid real relationships in the hope of living in a fluffy-white-cloud-filled world.

People who fall in love with everyone they meet often feel that there's something missing in themselves — a gap that only being in love can fill. This can lead to them being a demanding partner expecting perfection, a clingy partner who is terrified of you living your own life in case it makes you go off them or a hot and cold partner, who's wonderfully effusive to start with and then backs off once the reality of the relationship kicks in.

That said, it could just be that your man has got lucky and made good choices in his previous partners. Only you can judge which is the case, but it's best to protect your-self by not getting too carried away – moving in with each other, getting married or suchlike – until you're at least a year into a relationship. Well, come on, that's good advice even if you are with the person of your dreams.

Jan's story: He made me feel like a goddess – then left

Colin and I were friends for a few years before we got together. He'd flirted with me since we first met but I'd been attached, then heartbroken, so it took a long while of us knowing each other before I was remotely in a place to even consider dating him.

Once we did get together things moved at rocket speed. He told me that he loved me the first time we had sex, and I said that I felt the same way. He was so overwhelming with his declarations of love that I got carried along by his enthusiasm. I said things were moving fast for me but he said that I'd just been unlucky before. Whenever he'd been with someone serious, things had been just as fast with them. If I'd thought about it I'd have pointed out that he split up with all of them so it wasn't that good a guide, but I was enjoying being loved.

Then I got ill. I had a breast cancer scare and needed him by my side for all the tests. He came with me but his mood changed. He stopped buying me silly little presents, holding my hand in public, texting me just to say he was thinking about me, even kissing me other than in a perfunctory way. Just when I needed him most, he backed off. Luckily, the tests were all clear but I split up with him soon after. Now I wouldn't trust a man who got so keen so quickly. It was just too good to be true.

He refuses to tell you anything about his past

While everyone has a right to privacy, there's a certain amount of information it's only fair to expect to share, such as roughly how many partners you've had, when you became single, how long it took you to get over your ex — anything that could affect the relationship that you're in. If a man refuses to share even the basics, it suggests that he's either a total commitment-phobe or he's got something to hide. He's fine for a fling but anything more than this will probably mean trouble.

If you've been with your partner for a while and aren't prepared to bail out on the relationship just because he hasn't told you about his past, don't be tempted to try to find out about it on your own by asking his mates or snooping around, That's only likely to make him close up even more, as explained later in the book. Instead, try to find out why he's such a private person. Perhaps he grew up in a large family and everyone knew what everyone else was doing so now he's making up for it. Maybe there's something in his past that he's scared to tell you in case you leave him, such as having children, or homosexual relationships. All you can do is reassure your partner that you love him no matter what – as long as you really mean it – in the hope that he'll feel accepted enough to open up. Be warned: convincing a private person to share is a long job and could take you years.

Kirsty's story: He keeps himself to himself

I've been with Jamie for four years now, but all I know about his exes is that he had one girlfriend for three years when he was in his 20s and a few flings after that. When we first met, I asked him lots of questions but he'd just clam up and sulk if I tried to do any digging. It was really frustrating – I thought he'd got something to hide and couldn't see what the big deal was. I was happy to tell him everything about my past so it seemed like the relationship was one-sided. I was getting close to splitting up with him when he told me he wanted to introduce me to his mother. I was really surprised, given his general levels of secrecy about his life – I thought he didn't want to share anything with me.

When I met her I suddenly realised why he was like he was. She's the nosiest woman I've ever met. She asked me where I got my clothes from and where I got my hair cut within minutes of meeting me, which I thought was her being nice and trying to make me feel comfortable. But as the day progressed she got increasingly pushy. When Jamie was out of the room she asked me if we'd started having sex and other things that are even more personal. It seemed really inappropriate and I excused myself to go to the loo to escape from her questioning. After that day I could see why Jamie had such a horror of talking about himself – I can only imagine the hell he had to deal with growing up. I stopped asking him questions and, over time, he started opening up of his own accord. He's never going to win any 'Talkative man of the year' awards but I do feel a lot closer to him now when he does share something with me because I know how hard it must be for him to do it.

He doesn't talk much about his exes, though he's mentioned a couple of positive and negative anecdotes in passing

Result. He sounds pretty sorted. Either that or he's lying. Sorry, but I can't have you getting too smug now, can I?

And the rest...

Once you know what your man's ex-style says about him, you can make an assessment about whether he's the man for you. If your man's only behaved badly with one ex, don't assume he'll behave in exactly the same way with you as he did with them. Every relationship is different and his actions could be down to the way that his ex treated him, rather than an innate part of his relationship-map. That said, if there's a pattern of negative behaviour, or if you find out that your man hit his ex or otherwise abused her, it's worth giving him a wide berth. Some risks just aren't worth taking, no matter how loved-up you feel.

Even if you decide the future looks bright with your man, there are still a couple more problems that could come your way...

He's a jealousy creator

There are some men that actually encourage you to be jealous. If you're in this situation, you need to nip it in the bud as early as possible if you're ever going to have a successful relationship with him. Otherwise you'll end up feeling like a bunny boiler, and he'll drag your self-esteem down to his pitiful levels.

Some of the signs that your man is a jealousy creator include:

- Constantly comparing you to his exes and mentioning how great they were.
- Going out with exes (and female friends) and being secretive about it.
- Having a screen saver of a hot woman, who you later find out is his ex.
- Never committing to seeing you until the last minute, or cancelling on you just before a date so that you're never entirely sure where you stand.
- Taking an age to reply to messages you send him.

If you put up with this kind of behaviour, it will only get worse. Instead, if you don't want to dump him, you need to play him at his own game. Whenever he mentions his exes, make a joke of it to show that it doesn't affect you — for example, 'Oh yes, Mandy — isn't she the one that won the Nobel Peace Prize aged 17, was a supermodel and co-wrote the Kama Sutra?' Either that or just ignore it. If your man doesn't get a rise out of you then he'll soon get bored and stop such petty behaviour.

If his trick is being secretive about going out with his exes, just do the same. It's not big or clever but it'll soon wind him up and when he challenges you about it, you can say, 'God, you're right — let's agree to tell each other if we're going out with an ex, and explain what went on afterwards.' Because he's the one that brought the topic up, he won't get to complain about it, but you won't have to look as if you're being possessive.

You can use a similar trick with the screen saver — just set your own computer up with a pic of a hot man who may or may not be your ex and be ambiguous about it when questioned. He'll soon revert to having a screen saver that's a landscape rather than a foxy woman. And if he cancels dates on you last minute, do the same. Say to him, 'Sorry, I didn't think it was confirmed, given that you've cancelled the last few nights out we've had, so I arranged to go out with someone else.' Often, people can only see how bad their own behaviour is when they have to suffer it from someone else.

Don't beat your man up too much about being a jealousy creator. It stems — as most negative traits do — from insecurity. Once he starts to feel better about himself, he should stop behaving in such an immature manner. Reassure your bloke that he's gorgeous, hot in bed and an all-round top chap and he's likely to behave in a much better way towards you.

He dated Little Miss Perfect

And then there's the small matter of the 'perfect ex' – a woman your man dated in the past who, as far as you're concerned, is Mata Hari, Kate Moss, Jenna Jameson and Nigella Lawson all rolled into one. Unless your man talks about her all the time, the main problem here is your own insecurity. You're focusing on all her good points, probably ignoring your own attributes into the bargain, and forgetting the most important thing: she's his ex. If he wanted to be with her (or vice versa) then they wouldn't have split up.

That said, some men use a perfect ex as a way to drive down your self-esteem. If your man mentions his perfect ex whenever you do something that he doesn't like he may be falling into this trap (often subconsciously, so it doesn't mean he's a total bastard – just that he's insecure and immature). He's using her so-called perfection as a way to control you – but if he really thought she was that great then why did they split up? Either he's lying about exactly how great she was or she dumped him, in which case she's not exactly the perfect woman for him.

An even worse sign is if your man mentions his perfect ex when you're feeling great about yourself – say, you've spent ages getting ready to go out for an evening with him and are certain you look fab – and he says something along the lines of, 'Oh, Jess had a top like that, although she filled it out a bit more than you do.' A man who does this is toxic and is almost certainly still pining over his ex. Make the first time he comes up with such nonsense the last date you ever have with him.

His ex wants him back

And then there are problems that aren't caused by your man at all. One of the most common is the ex who's still in love with your man. If she's a bunny boiler, chances are he'll hate it just as much as you do, if not more (unless he's a totally insecure freak who needs constant validation from everyone he's ever dated). With any luck, this ex will vanish over the course of time. He'll get fed up with her behaviour because clinginess is hardly an appealing character trait. Either than or she'll get a new boyfriend and stop trying to get her hooks into yours. However, until this happens, you have to put up with her nonsense.

A woman who's still obsessed by her ex may do any of the following: call him every day, often repeatedly and until the early hours; turn up to see him unannounced; blog about him; tell people she's still going out with him; spread rumours about you; spread rumours about him; try to befriend you then start making digs about him/introduce poisonous thoughts to the relationship; try to seduce him; boil his bunny rabbit; something more creative. All in all, it's a joy to be a part of. And sadly, unless she turns stalker and you can get the law involved, you just have to grin and bear it.

It does make sense for your man to have a talk with her so that she's absolutely sure of the situation and doesn't have any scope for thinking that she could get him back. However, there's no guarantee, even if your man does try to clear things up, that she'll go away. Often, the only way to deal with this is to sit it out and wait for her to get over him in her own time. Don't hate her too much though. She's only acting in this way because she feels hurt, and we've all been there – even if we haven't acted in such a bad way – so give her a bit of sympathy. You never know what her motivations are: and your man might not be telling you the whole story…

Mona's story: He said she was a nutter but I didn't realise how far she'd go

Gary kept on getting calls and texts from his ex when he and I first met. He said things had ended ages ago between them, he didn't want to be with her and she was just a stalker. I thought it was a bit odd but I decided not to pry too much – it was his problem, not mine.

Over coming months the calls kept going on though – sometimes five or six times a day. One day, just over six months into our relationship, I decided to look through his mobile phone to see if I could get a better idea of what was going on. When I looked through his phone call log at first I was relieved to see that he was telling the truth – although she called him all the time, he never called her back. He'd also got loads of texts from her saying she loved him. At first I thought it was just her refusing to let go but when I looked at his 'sent' items he was telling her that he loved her too. I was gutted and couldn't believe I'd been so stupid.

I confronted him and he said that he only sent her messages like that to keep her off his back – if he told her it was over, she phoned him all the time. I didn't really believe him – she called him all the time as it was – but thought I'd give him the benefit of the doubt because I loved him. He made it all sound so convincing.

Then one night we had a row about something else and he stormed out. I tried to call him to sort things out but he wouldn't answer the phone to me and he ignored my texts for a week. That weekend he called me drunk and said that he loved me though, so I wasn't sure whether we'd really split up.

In desperation, I called his mum to ask her if she could shed any light on things – we'd always got on well and I thought I'd get the truth out of her. It turned out that he'd been seeing his 'ex' the first six months of our relationship and had only dumped her when I found his texts to her. His mum said that he really cared about me and I was much better for him than his ex, but there was no way I was going to get back together with him after that. I can't believe I was such a fool. I thought Gary's ex was stalking him but actually she was just being his girlfriend – when I thought that was what I was to him.

His ex is clingy

The most dangerous type of man-fixated ex is the one who says that she just wants to be friends with him, and is convincing enough that he believes her, yet somehow always happens to wear skimpy clothes whenever they go out, or calls him at 1 am to see if he'll rescue her from a club she's stranded at, or has a crisis she needs his help with whenever the pair of you have got a romantic weekend planned. Sometimes it's not even that obvious: she might ask to stay over at his place one night when you happen to be out of town, or invite him to her birthday party but not you 'because of numbers'.

First off, check that you're not ascribing dubious motives to her behaviour because you're a jealous loon. The occasional cry for help or glammed-up night is nothing to feel threatened by. Even mild flirting could be an accidental thing – some people are naturally flirtatious – though if it makes you feel uncomfortable, it is worth raising the issue (politely) with his ex. If she's a nice person she'll try to moderate her behaviour. If she doesn't, or makes out that you're making a fuss about nothing, chances are she really is after your man, in which case you need to have a chat with him about the situation. While it's not on to ask a man to stop seeing one of his mates just because he used to get it on with her, it is acceptable asking him not to spend time alone with a woman who's clearly trying to get into his pants.

Again, don't be too harsh on this woman. Sure, she might have the good taste to fancy your bloke, but they split up and he's subsequently chosen you, so there's no need to get insecure about her. The behaviour she's exhibiting comes from her own insecurities – she feels nervous about being on her own so needs a man to look after her, even if he's 'someone else's'. You may find that befriending her helps to take the stress out of the situation as she'll be less likely to see your man as her property, and may well feel guilty about her own behaviour once she realises how lovely you are. Given the shortage of desirable single men out there, you could be kind and let her borrow your man on occasion – as long as she promises to keep her hands (and other body parts) strictly to herself.

Beth's story: I made a new friend

I knew about Charlotte from day one of my relationship with Cliff. He'd dated her a couple of years before and they'd stayed friends ever since. He met up with her every Thursday night and she'd often call him out the blue to ask for help building flat-pack furniture, fixing her car or fixing her computer. If I'm honest I was a bit jealous at first but he said there was nothing going on and I believed him. After we'd been with each other for a month I asked him to introduce me to her, and he did. At first it felt a bit uncomfortable sitting there with him and her but after a couple of glasses of wine she and I started talking and soon poor old Cliff was being totally ignored while Charlotte and I talked 19 to the dozen. Now I think that she and I are almost as good friends as her and Cliff. I know she's not after my man – she just likes having someone that she can call on to help her out, which is fair enough. However, I am thinking of setting her up with a male mate of mine who I think she'll get on with. He's handy around the house so he'd be able to help her and she wouldn't need to keep borrowing Cliff.

It's impossible to stop a man's exes from entering your relationship in any way, shape or form. However, with a bit of effort, it is possible to guard against them having a negative effect on your relationship. All you then need to do is deal with your own exes...

Ten reasons to be glad about his exes

1. They helped train him out of some of his worst boy bad habits before you ever met him.
2. He's had a chance to experiment with other women so is less likely to feel the need to sow his wild oats.
3. If it hadn't been for them, his sex education would have come courtesy of the pages from a porn mag he found fluttering loose in his local park, and the whisperings of his mates who'd 'done it'...
4. ...and you don't have to deal with the nightmare of taking his virginity.
5. One of his exes is bound to have done something that he's classified as 'bunny boiler' so you're unlikely to be the worst girlfriend he's ever had.
6. He's had the most horrific vestiges of bad dress sense beaten out of him.
7. If it wasn't for them, you'd be the first woman to ever meet his mum – and have to deal with cutting the apron strings on your own.

8. Because of his exes, your man's had 'dating practice' and has at least a vague clue about how women want to be treated (whether or not he does it is another matter entirely).

9. None of them were right for him, and because of that, he's ended up with you.

10. Every ex he's had has formed part of his character, so you're dating the sum of their parts on top of his original personality.

Chapter 4

Dealing with *Your* Exes

So, you're well and truly over any of your exes. You've found a new man. You've dealt with any issues relating to your partner's exes. Well done you. It's all too easy to assume that things will only get better from this point onwards but that's a big mistake. If you get complacent, you're heading for a fall. You see, there's also the small matter of *your* exes to deal with. Just because you've moved on, it doesn't mean that they're out of your life forever. They may just be lurking in your subconscious, ready to leap out and ambush you once your next relationship starts to get serious, so you need to keep an eye out for the dangers that are around.

There are numerous ways that an ex can mess up your future relationships. They might leave you with enough baggage to keep every luggage terminal at a major city airport busy. You could find yourself telling a new man all about your ex, only to find yourself getting into a row because he either doesn't agree that your ex was the bastard scum of Satan, or because he thinks you talk about the ex in overly glowing terms. Your ex might deliberately try to sabotage your relationship. Or it could even be that you get into a relationship, only to realise a few months in that, actually, for all you thought you were 'cured', you're not over your ex after all.

And then there's your man's reaction to your exes. Just as you may feel insecure about some of the women in his past, he might get an understandable pang of jealousy about the men that you've dated. A jealous man can be just as much of a nightmare to deal with as a jealous woman, and you need to know how much is an acceptable level of jealousy, and what falls into the category of 'out-of-order behaviour'. Spending your entire relationship defending yourself against accusations of infidelity, or coping with constant digs about your past can be an easy way to shred your self-esteem, and that's no fun for anyone.

Luckily, all of these problems have a solution. By facing up to them as soon as they surface, you can stop them from getting to scary relationship-killing levels. And if you're already a long way down that path? Don't worry, you can still turn back, take a different path and get things going in the right direction again.

Your ex and your new man

Like it or not, men have just as many insecurities as women do and your new man may well be worried about how he matches up to the guys you've dated before. He might also want to find out what you're like as a girlfriend once the honeymoon period wears off, and knowing about the way you treated your ex can be a handy way for him to learn more about you.

As a result, even if you're no longer in contact with your ex, don't be surprised if your new man wants to know about your relationship history. You may find him asking tricky questions about exactly what went wrong with your previous relationships. He might inquire about your ex's bedroom talent, or sexual things that you've tried with other men before. It's highly likely that he'll be curious about the number of exes you've had, or at least the amount of people you've slept with in the past.

Even if your new man doesn't ask any of these questions, there's a reasonable chance that you'll find yourself proffering the information unprompted when you're drunk or in a classically girlie 'over-sharing' kind of mood – which is where things can start to go wrong. Unfortunately, women seem to find it necessary to talk about their exes as a way of analysing previous mistakes they've made and preventing themselves from making said mistakes again. Or hell, it could even be because we want to talk about something that no man can claim to know more about than we do.

Bella's story: I'm an open book

I don't really mind anything being asked about my exes – what is there to hide? It's something/someone that has been part of your life and I think it helps to understand a person when you know about their past. I also think it makes you closer and avoids any surprises in the future.

Although Bella's approach may seem logical, there are better ways to get close to a partner than sharing stories about previous lovers. The potential for things to go wrong if you choose the 'tell each other everything' route is just too immense. If you complain about your ex, you'll run the risk of sounding like an embittered harridan, and your man may well wonder how you'd describe him if the pair of you were to split up. This is particularly likely at the start of a relationship if you're still licking your wounds from a bloke who dumped you. (Yes, OK, ideally you should wait until all the wounds are healed before moving on to anyone else, but in the real world, that doesn't always happen – particularly given that lots of women subscribe to the 'get over one man by getting under another' approach).

Rob's story: She was too much

I wanted this woman the second I saw her. She was dancing on her own on an empty dance floor, not caring that everyone was looking at her but not looking like she was playing to the crowd either. She was just lost in her own little world. She was wearing a dress made out of some sort of floaty material and she had a cracking figure – all curves and long legs: I felt like I could watch her all night. As it was, I decided to seize my chance and join her so I could beat all the other guys to pulling her.

After we danced together I offered her a drink and we started talking. A couple of beers later and I got the guts to ask her whether she was single. What a mistake. She said that she was but then started telling me all about her ex, who she'd split up with a few months before. I tried to change the subject but she insisted on giving me all the gory details – the rows they'd had (almost word for word) the insults he'd thrown at her – she even asked my opinion on whether she'd said the right things when they were arguing. I was bored out of my mind. I didn't ask for her number and I'm glad I didn't. If I had I think I'd still be listening to her droning endlessly on and on and on.

Conversely, if you tell your new man that your ex was good at anything at all, no matter how insignificant it may seem to you, chances are it'll deliver a bit of a sting to new man's ego – no man wants to think that he's competing against your past. And if he's really immature he could well end up taking it out on you (OK, you could use this as a test to weed out the dross but do you really want to waste your time testing a man to see if he's good enough for you?).

Emily's story: They're scared of my exes

I do a fair amount of work in the adult industry. As a result, I've dated a couple of porn stars over the years. I never saw it as a big deal. As far as I'm concerned, they're just normal men (OK, well-endowed ones but I've dated men outside the industry who were just as big). But men seem to see it differently. If I let slip I've dated porn stars they seem to think they've got to prove themselves with bedroom gymnastics and a million different positions. The worst time was when I was watching a porn film on cable with an ex and I was a bit the worse for wear. I blurted out, 'I've had him,' just as one of the guys started pumping away. Sure, it wasn't the most intelligent thing to say, but I didn't see it as any big deal. My boyfriend, on the other hand, sulked all night and refused to have sex with me. I don't see why porn stars are so threatening to men, but I try to avoid telling men about my porn exes now.

And then there's the breadth of your history to consider. If you say you've had a lot of exes, your new partner may well find himself looking at every bloke you pass in the supermarket, wondering whether they've known the joys of your flesh. And if you say that you were a virgin when you met, he'll assume you're lying (because, well, you probably are).

So what exactly should you share with your partner about your exes? Easy: the bare minimum. The only information that you need to impart is anything that could affect your new man's life. If your ex was obsessive and is now stalking you, it's worth warning your new partner about it so that he can be on the lookout for anyone following him or generally behaving in a threatening way. Should you have contracted an incurable STI (or one that you're currently undergoing treatment for), it's only fair to let your new man know before he gets into your pants (yes, even if it means potentially blowing the chance of you getting it on with him – it's not fair to remove the choice about taking a sexual health risk from his hands due to lack of information). And if you've dated your new man's best mate, boss or dad, it's probably worth telling him sooner rather than later (and resigning yourself to the fact that this relationship probably isn't going to go anywhere).

Sally's story: I had a secret

When I met Luke, I thought he was gorgeous – floppy brown hair, big eyes and a ridiculously hot body. We were at a formal dinner party, sitting next to each other, and got on really well. We exchanged numbers and I went home feeling excited. It was only when I looked at his card when I got home (in that soppy 'getting far too excited far too soon' way) that I realised I'd copped off with his brother a few years before (he has an unusual surname and I had a vague recollection, once things clicked into place, that my ex had mentioned a brother with the name that was on the card in front of me). I didn't know what to do – I mean, how often do you exchange surnames when making a date? It wasn't as if it was intentional. I decided that I'd wait to see how things progressed rather than confessing on our first date. I didn't want to ruin the mood and I was pretty sure Luke wouldn't be impressed.

The first date went really well, and I felt in even more of a quandary – how exactly could I say, 'Err,

Luke, a few years back I had a doomed one-nighter with your brother. I was going through a bad time and it was a huge mistake but I'm sorted now and you're lovely'? I just couldn't see the conversation panning out.

As it was, Luke's brother ungallantly did the job for me. On date two, I was sitting there with Luke, chatting away, when he blurted out, 'So, I was talking to my brother at the weekend. He said you fucked him.'

I tried to explain, succeeded in over-explaining and lost a potential boyfriend all in the space of five minutes. Not one of the proudest moments of my life…

However, unless you have something significant that you need to tell your man about your ex, try really hard to keep your mouth shut. It doesn't mean that you're a closed individual or unwilling to share yourself with your partner. It's just being discreet.

If your new man asks you a direct question about your ex, think about any benefit that could come from you sharing the information he's requesting. If there's no benefit, evade, evade, evade. A simple, 'I don't want to talk about him – you're so much better,' followed by a deep kiss will usually distract a man enough to take his mind off it.

Should *you* really feel a need to talk about your ex, call one of your friends rather than sharing any info with your man. A friend will be able to have a conversation about every infinitesimal detail of your ex without it damaging your new relationship (though don't make a habit of it – for heaven's sake, your mate's probably just helped you get over your ex and there's only so much self-obsession that should be allowed to creep into a friendship).

As a general guide, just use your common sense to figure out how much you should tell your man about your ex, and the way that you should say it. Imagine how you'd feel if your man started telling you about his ex's great job in PR, her part-time modelling career or her ability to eat whatever she wanted without putting on an ounce of weight. Would it make you feel good? So do you really need to mention that one of your exes was a racing car driver, or that you once had a man whose cock was so big you couldn't get your hand around it? Even if the positive attributes of your exes aren't that extreme, they could still batter a weak man's ego. And surely you have better things to talk to your new squeeze about anyway?

Anca's story: I tell them nothing

I don't share anything with my partners about exes really. The men I go out with give me the impression that they would prefer to forget that I ever went out with anyone else, let alone had sex with them. I'm not always that comfortable with their history either. I don't want an inexperienced virgin but too much detail can conjure up images that are no less likely to make me feel jealous than if they cheated. If a man shared details about sex with other women I would immediately be put off him, as he'd be sure to do it about me. I'd then feel like I was being judged by a committee of him and all his future girlfriends. Oh, and asking about numbers is a waste of time. Everyone lies!

As Anca identifies, it's not just sharing specifics with your ex that can lead to trouble. There's also the generic numbers question – and when a man asks, 'How many people have you slept with?' there is no right answer. If your total is higher than the guy you're dating, chances are he'll judge you for being slutty, no matter how 'new-age guy' he claims to be (unless he's staggeringly mature and secure – and that's a very rare man to find). If your figure is lower than his, either he'll think you're lying or you'll feel insecure that he's got way more experience than you. Yes, it's a clichéd response in both cases, and isn't the way that either of you should respond if you're totally happy with yourself, but clichés exist because they're true.

There are various ways to deal with the numbers question. If you're certain that your man's less experienced than you, then you can try eliciting his number then claiming that your own number is half his (minus two if you don't want it to look too obvious – and just in case he's gone for the male trick of doubling his real number to sound more 'manly'). However, only try this if you're a damned convincing liar.

Alternatively – and far better – tell the truth ... kind of. Tell him, 'I haven't had unprotected sex with anyone since I last got tested.' OK, to be able to do this you do need to practise safer sex and get tested if you do end up taking any risks at any point – but you should be doing that anyway to make sure you don't get any horrid diseases. Look on the bright side – if you go with this option you've got a good way to get out of an awkward question as well as a healthy body.

Or you could go for the old, 'Darling, numbers don't matter to me – people do – and you're the only person I want to have sex with now,' line, if you think you can say it without giggling.

Similarly, if your man asks about how many times you've been in love before, avoid sharing the details. It *is* acceptable to give an honest answer (assuming you don't tend to think you've fallen in love with everyone you've ever so much as held hands with) but there's really no need at all to explain how you fell in love, where you fell in love and why you fell in love with the ex. It may sound obvious but you'd be amazed how many women make the mistake of believing their partner will want to know every bit of their relationship history in order to know the 'real them'. Think about it – would you really want to hear every last detail about how your partner fell for his ex? Thought not.

Generally, when it comes down to sharing information about your exes, never make the mistake of believing that true love requires total honesty. Little white lies make relationships run smoothly – your boyfriend *is* the best lover you've ever had, he *does* have the best penis you've ever seen and you've *never* fantasised about any of your exes since you've met him. Honest. It's just better that way.

Sweet nothings

The above is all very easy if you're in a calm and rational state of mind. However, there's a special word of warning should you choose to speak while having sex. It's all too easy to mention you particularly like a kinky sex act, or ask your man to change his technique, only for him to ask, 'So how did you find out you like that?' This is a tough question to evade. Whatever you do, avoid answering, 'Oh, Darren took me to Torture Garden one night and ended up spanking me in front of a room of strangers – it was hot' (not least because it may scare a vanilla guy). The second you mention another man in relation to your sex life, your partner will find himself picturing it. And unless he's particularly wild, chances are he'll find it a massive turn-off.

Instead, you need to remember this simple but vital answer: 'I read about it in a magazine.' This is how you learned everything about sex. No other man has ever touched you in the way that your current boyfriend does. You wouldn't even dream of getting dirty with anyone in your past. OK, faking virginity is going too far, but by obfuscating over exactly where you learned to deliver the perfect prostate massage followed by some tromboning and one-on-one bukkake (look it up – it's far too rude to explain here) is only going to save you grief in the long run.

Susan's story: My dirty talking dilemma

I've always been into talking dirty. I find that it really helps me to get off and luckily, I've had quite a few boyfriends that were as into it as I am. My most recent ex, Sam, in particular, was pure filth. There was nothing he wouldn't say – even though he'd never do half the things he suggested and in reality, neither would I – but we both got really into saying the filthiest things we could think of, no-holds-barred. I got used to it, and was just as dirty as him. I'm getting wet just thinking about it…

Sadly, we had to split up because his visa expired. A month or so later I started dating Mick. He's a lovely guy but nothing like as obscene as Sam. I don't mind – I can keep my own mental dialogue going while we have sex without needing to have him join in. But the other night I was really enjoying what he was doing and got a bit carried away. I came out with a stream of filth that Sam would have loved. Mick stopped what he was doing, horrified, and I realised what I'd done. I was so embarrassed. I explained I didn't mean it but I'm sure Mick thinks I'm a bit of a weirdo now and I'm not sure what to do about it.

All the above rules apply doubly if you're drunk. If you decide there's something that you really want to share with your man but you've had more than a couple of glasses of wine, write it down and look at it in the morning to decide whether it's still something that you want to admit to. Chances are you'll want to burn the paper right away and will be grateful that you didn't just blurt out what was on your mind.

Boundaries, boundaries

But it's not just over-sharing that can cause problems. Jealousy is an incredibly common emotion, for men as well as women. And it's particularly rife now that men and women are so much more likely to be friends, so that your lover has more scope to get all testosteroney about your muscle-bound best boy mate (who you wouldn't sleep with in a million years). As such, it's worth agreeing boundaries with your partner so that you don't inadvertently end up hurting him (or vice versa). Try to empathise with your man: imagine what would make you feel jealous then endeavour not to do anything that you think would be upsetting.

However, there are both acceptable and unacceptable boundaries. It's all too easy for a partner to get annoyed with you for staying friends with an ex, purely because of their own insecurities. While it's not acceptable for a man to ban you from hanging out with your ex – unless you commit infidelity with said ex – it is perfectly within their rights to set a few ground rules. After all, if you want to dictate terms of 'ex behaviour' to your man, it's only fair that he gets to return the favour. Here are some that you really shouldn't refuse:

You shouldn't flirt with your ex

It doesn't matter how 'naturally flirtatious' you claim to be: flirting with an ex in front of your new partner is just plain bad manners. If you're so out of control when it comes to your emotions that you're unable to tweak your behaviour so that you don't hurt someone you're professing to care about, you need to get some therapy and, frankly, grow up.

Should your man accuse you of flirting with your ex when you're certain that you haven't been, try to find a third party who can give you an honest opinion about your actions: a best friend is a good choice, as long as she won't lie to protect your feelings and/or doesn't hate your new man.

Flirting with other people – whether you've dated them or not – when you're with your partner shows a worrying level of neediness. You really shouldn't need that much convincing that you're an attractive person. Try to get your self-esteem from within. Or hell, go against what all the manuals advise and get it from the bloke you're dating. It's better than needing it from every man in the room.

You shouldn't share a bed with your ex

As a single woman, you may well have got used to sharing a bed with exes (or other male friends) if you go out for an evening together and can't be bothered to get a cab home when it gets late. While this can be a perfectly acceptable way to get affection when you're single, once you're attached all that late-night snuggling has to end. It doesn't matter that nothing sexual happens. You're still being physically intimate with one man when you're dating someone else, and unless you've established that it's something your partner doesn't mind, it's just not on.

In fact even if your bloke says that it's OK, you're still treading on dodgy ground. It's not exactly uncommon for a snuggle to turn into something altogether cosier, from which it's all too easy for things to 'crop up'. And what goes up all too often leads to being gone down on.

Instead, get your mate to see you home or into a cab at the end of the night. It might be a bit more of a pain but if it protects your relationship then it's worth it. And if the idea of giving up nights in your ex's bed for your new man is simply too hard to bear? Guess what – you're not over him. Deal with your feelings before things get any more complicated.

Asking too much

There are also boundaries that your man may try to impose, which are utterly out of order. If he asks you to do any of the following, you're well within your rights to tell him where to get off:

You must not see your ex

This is scary and controlling behaviour, indicating someone who, at best, is chronically insecure, and at worst, is domestically violent or a stalker in the making. The only exception to this is if you've cheated on your partner with said ex. In that situation, they're entirely within their rights to make you stop seeing them, assuming, of course, that they don't dump you for cheating.

You must tell me everything about your ex

What you share about your ex is entirely up to you. Unless something about your ex is going to have a direct impact on your partner – say, they gave you an incurable STI – there's nothing that they need to know.

You mustn't talk about your ex

Similarly, placing an outright ban on you talking about anyone you've ever dated before is overly controlling behaviour. If an ex's name crops up on (a relevant) occasion, there's no reason that it should make a sane and balanced guy feel obsessively jealous. That said, it is fair enough for your partner to say that he doesn't want to hear your stories about the wonderful romantic time you had with your ex, or about your illegal-in-most-states-noisy-back-scratching-fluid-soaked-and-filthy sex sessions. In fact you should ask yourself why you would possibly want to share that sort of information with him. Do you really have no empathy?

You can't compare me to your ex

OK, deep down almost every woman compares the man she's with now to the man she was with before him – and quite possibly, every man before that too. But the last thing you want to do is tell a man that to his face. Few things are more likely to make a man's ego (and penis) shrivel than the words, 'That's just what my ex used to do

— you're so like him.' After all, you're no longer with your ex, so what does that tell your man about his chances of having a successful relationship with you? More to the point, what exactly does he gain by knowing that he's similar to someone else that you once knew but he, in all probability, has never met? So, the trick here is to carry on doing exactly what you always have — but keep your mouth well and truly shut.

Apart from anything else, if your new man really is similar to your ex, it could well be down to your own baggage, and certainly isn't worth bringing up in the heat of the moment. If, on closer analysis alone, you realise that your current bloke does share a number of your ex's negative points, think about why it is you've gone for someone with the same traits again. If you're annoyed with a guy for being broke, when you're always attracted to aspiring musicians, or you're wound up because a man's controlling, when you were mostly drawn to him because of his wallet, it could be that the similarities are down to the men that you pick. And that's something that only you can change. Unless or until you do, keep those comparisons to yourself.

Help, I need somebody!

And then there's the problem of relying on exes for emotional support. If you're going through grief with your new man, is it OK to call on a friendly ex to help you deal with the problem?

As a general rule, no. By inviting your ex back into your life to help you deal with any emotional hassles you're going through, you're allowing them to become too involved in your life. Once a relationship ends, it's unfair to expect your previous partner to deal with your crises – hell, that's what friends are for (or you could even try being self-reliant – you never know, you might like it).

If you quiz an ex about relationship problems you're having with your new partner, don't be surprised if it turns into a character assassination, where they point out all the things that you did wrong when you went out with them. Alternatively, you may find your cry for help being misinterpreted as an opportunity to try to get into your pants. Your ex may even flat out decline to give you any help with your problem – which will probably make you feel even worse than you did to start with.

However, there are some times when an ex's opinion can come in handy: when you want to figure out whether your partner's done something wrong or whether you're just overreacting in a way that you suspect you have before; or when your ex is the person who knows you more intimately than anyone else, you've stayed on good terms and you need someone who is going to be totally honest with you (rather than do the kind friend thing of merely offering a shoulder to cry on and telling you that you're right). If you've stayed friends with your ex and are certain he's going to give you an objective response to any questions you ask, rather than automatically responding with, 'Well, you were always a nightmare to deal with,' or 'He would say that – I told you that he was never good enough for you,' then you can give it a go. Just don't blame me if it all goes wrong.

Jon's story: We bounced things off each other

One of my exes and I used to play agony aunt to each other. We knew each other really well – our strengths and weaknesses and (of course) our annoying habits that would tend to drive our new partners crazy. And we could be very straight and direct with each other. I've always been grateful for this and never thought it was the wrong thing to do. Although one time we did sleep together while I was dating someone else. But that didn't come out of a support session. It came out of a bag of weed and a *Cosmo* sex survey. I think she may have planned it in advance...

If you do ask an ex for advice, it is worth being wary that you don't get too dependent though. It's all too easy to go from crying on an ex's shoulder to snuggling up on the sofa to pulling each other's clothes off and getting hot and heavy.

Emma's story: He went from a helping hand to wandering hands

Andrew and I had a lot of history. We met at university, dated, he cheated, I discovered he'd thought we were only seeing each other casually, I went mental, we fell out with each other then became friends again a year later. After all that we ended up seeing each other in a non-committal way for three years – after I'd left university and moved to a big city. Eventually we'd been seeing each other exclusively for a year so I asked if he'd make it official so we could be boyfriend and girlfriend. He said no and I said I needed a break from seeing him so that I could stop feeling so emotionally involved.

Then I met Stewart. In hindsight, I was still on the rebound from Andrew – it was only three weeks after we stopped seeing each other – but I fell head over heels in love regardless – or perhaps because of it. Andrew refused to speak to me from that day forwards.

Fast-forward a year and Stewart and I were going through problems. The initial passion had faded long before and we were starting to annoy each other on a daily basis – possibly because we'd moved in together, which added lots of domestic and financial pressure to the relationship. Stewart went off sex entirely and no matter what I did, I couldn't get him interested again.

At this point, Andrew resurfaced – turning up randomly on my doorstep as if nothing had happened. We went for a drink, I introduced him to Stewart, they got on and everything was good again.

A few weeks later, Andrew asked me to go to stay with him for the weekend. I thought it was innocent and Stewart was fine about it because I said we were just friends. I thought I was telling the truth.

When I turned up at Andrew's he dragged me straight out to the pub and we proceeded to get royally hammered. Back at his place we carried on drinking and soon, all my worries about Stewart were coming out. One minute I was crying and the next I was trying to kiss him.

To his credit, he stopped me, lit me a cigarette, turned the lights on and asked if I was sure about what I was doing. I felt so undesired by Stewart that the idea of someone finding me attractive was compelling, so I said yes. I don't feel proud of myself but I'd have probably gone mad if I'd have gone for much longer feeling so unsexy. One thing led to another and the next morning we were most definitely post-coital.

I stayed with Stewart – though we've split up now – and stayed friends with Andrew too (with the occasional dalliance when things were going wrong with Stewart – something I'm ashamed of now, as I think I should have tried harder to work things out with him instead).

Years later I asked Andrew about that night, saying I was impressed with him for being so gentlemanly and giving me a chance to opt out. He confessed that he'd only invited me down because he wanted to seduce me. Now I'd think twice about asking an ex for advice – maybe if I hadn't confided in him I'd still be with Stewart. Ironically, I'm not even in contact with Andrew any more – when he got a serious girlfriend she banned him from seeing me, because she didn't like the idea of him being friends with an ex.

As you can see, approaching an ex to give you advice about your man can be fraught with peril (or at least the potential for copping off) so is best avoided. Unless that's what you want, in which case you're so not over your ex and you should go back to the beginning of the book and start reading from the Introduction again.

Pleased to meet you

And it's not just about *your* relationship with your ex. You may also face the joy of introducing your new man to your ex, should you run into him in the street. Or heaven forbid, actually arrange a social gathering that they're both going to be at (if you really want a happy birthday then why introduce trouble to the equation by doing such a silly thing?). This situation can be anything from mildly uncomfortable to excruciatingly hellish, depending on how unlucky you get. At best, they'll say hello politely and move swiftly on before any harm's done. At worst, they'll end up becoming best friends, and you'll spend the early hours of the morning panicking about them discussing you in detail, and realising that you tell every man you fuck that he's the first person to make you come so hard that you cry.

No matter how mature either of the guys is, it's highly likely that they'll get all alpha male when they first meet. In the case of the former 'hi and bye' approach watch out for mutual chest-puffing, and your boyfriend suddenly putting a possessive arm around your shoulders. In the latter scenario, don't be surprised if they end up discussing who has the biggest and most powerful car (ahem), comparing sporting achievements or name-dropping their accomplishments. Come on, if you were going to meet a boyfriend's ex you'd probably wear a push-up bra/miniskirt/tight jeans (depending on your best asset), and be as scintillating as you possibly could be, so don't get all smug and assume women are any better than men in this regard.

There's also the risk that your ex might try to sabotage your relationship with your new man by telling him lies (or unpleasant truths) about you when he meets him. If this happens, don't get angry or take the bait. Just say, 'Nice to see you. Anyway, we're late for dinner,' and leave, pulling your man firmly behind you. Defending yourself will sound, well, defensive to your new man, and that's never a good look. Afterwards, avoid any situations where your ex and your new man could collide: if someone tries hard enough to break a relationship, it can be worryingly successful so it's just not worth the risk. If your ex then goes out of his way to sabotage your relationship, meet up with him to talk things through and try to get 'closure'. He's clearly not over you yet. If that doesn't work, go back to Chapter 1 and treat him like a stalker ex. He has no right to try to mess up your life or be a part of it in any way now that you've split up.

Regardless of what happens when your man meets your ex, once you're out of the testosterone hell of the situation and on your own with your bloke, it is worth reassuring him how great he is: in particular how much better than your ex he is, focusing on any points you know he's insecure about. Don't tell obvious lies – saying that he's much better looking when your ex is a model and your new man's a double for Gollum, or that he's just as bright as your ex when said ex is a professor and your new man still moves his lips when he reads. Instead, focus on your man's positives while mildly criticising your ex — say that you love your bloke because he can hold a conversation that doesn't revolve around himself, or that he listens to you whereas, your ex droned on for years about Ancient Greek architecture. And if he's still tetchy, you could always mention that your ex was as well endowed and sexually proficient as a bromide-addicted gnat. It might be a tad unfair on your ex, but it's highly unlikely your man will ever be in a situation to discover whether your claims were a lie.

Lauren's story: They ignored me

I was dreading introducing Dave to my ex, Lee, but I felt that I had to because Lee and I stayed friends after we split and I see him quite a lot. Dave was OK about this but understandably wanted to check there wasn't anything more going on (he didn't say that, just said it'd be good to meet him as I spent so much time with him, but I'm not stupid). The problem is, Lee's quite flirty, and I was worried this might make Dave jealous. I asked him to tone it down and he told me not to be stupid – he wasn't that much of an idiot.

We arranged to meet up in a pub and I nervously introduced them, mentioning that Dave had just bought a new computer, because Lee works in IT and I figured they'd have some common ground. Then I did a cowardly thing and I went to the bar to get us drinks so I didn't have to sit through the uncomfortable conversation they were bound to end up having. What a mistake! When I got back they were talking about RAM this and gigabyte that. I couldn't get a word in edgeways. I spent the entire night staring into my drink and waiting for them to talk about something interesting but it never happened. When we got home, Dave couldn't understand why I was in such a bad mood. He didn't seem to realise that, much as I wanted them to get on, I didn't want them to ignore me entirely. Now, Dave sees Lee almost as much as I do – but when they go out together I stay at home so they can geek out without boring me rigid.

We already met...

There is one thing trickier than introducing your man to your ex: dealing with a new man who's already friends with your ex, and vice versa. The best way to cope with this, as with many things, is with foresight. If you know that a guy you fancy is mates with one of your exes, talk to said ex about the fact that you want to date his mate, and get his approval (or at least try) before any fluids are exchanged.

Don't be surprised if you meet resistance when having this conversation: it doesn't necessarily mean your ex is still hung up on you. Remember how insecure men can be. While you might think that asking your ex if you can date his mate is a thoughtful gesture borne out of politeness and a desire to spare his feelings at a later date, he may well panic at the idea of one of his mates dating you and finding out all his innermost secrets. If he has a tiny penis or bizarre fetish, he could be particularly scared that you'll tell all.

Reassure him that you'd never talk about an ex with a new man (less convincing if he knows about your ex with the penchant for Japanese schoolgirl panties, the guy who wanted to be locked in a wardrobe, and the one who yelled, 'Take my love-custard, baby,' at the point of climax, but still worth a go). A bit of flattery won't go amiss either – point out that friends tend to be similar to each other and his friend has some attributes that remind you of him, so obviously you find said mate hot.

If your man is really anti the idea of you dating his mate, do consider his feelings: friendship is more important than a casual relationship so if you don't think there's potential for something special with his mate, don't be mean and dick with their friendship. You wouldn't like it if your ex dated your best mate just because he thought she looked hot in a miniskirt, after all. However, if you think there is potential for a good relationship (or a fuck so staggeringly intense that it will live in your memory as anything but casual until the end of time) then don't let your ex stand in your way. It's your life, after all.

And then there's dealing with the new man. The big rule here is to avoid chatting about your ex/his mate with him. It will naturally make him feel torn if you spend an hour talking about the evil bastard who screwed your life up, who he knows better as, 'Gaz, that top bloke who always gets the drinks in.' Slagging off a guy's mates is never a way to endear yourself to him. Be discreet; don't go for public displays of affection if your ex is around (or ideally, ever – it's so tacky) and don't *ever* compare your new man to your ex, even (particularly) if telling him that his cock's bigger. You can't guarantee your relationship will last and, if it doesn't, your man may well tell you ex all the dirt that you shared, which really won't make you popular.

Return of the man

It's not just exes themselves that can cause problems: your psyche can do just as much damage. Sometimes, it's only when you start dating someone new that you realise you're not over your ex. You can be happily pootling along, genuinely thinking that your heartbreak is a thing of the past, bump into the new 'man of your dreams', feel all floaty and happy, wander around with a foolish grin on your face starting every sentence with, 'My new man says…' – and then, the second the honeymoon period fades and it starts looking like a real relationship is on the cards, get the urge to run a mile. You may find yourself comparing your new man to your ex. You might suddenly start getting nostalgic for the good times you shared with your ex. You may even start being mean to your new man because resentments from your previous relationship are still lurking in your subconscious like germs in a U-bend.

If you find yourself in this situation, you need to take a step back before making any hasty decisions. Spend a few days on your own rather than trying to get the magic back by being with your partner – don't make a big deal out of it, just say that you're busy. You need to ask yourself some serious questions without any distraction from your new man (it's a lot easier figuring out how you really feel when someone isn't blowing raspberries on your stomach).

Think hard: are you genuinely pining after your ex or is it just that your past experience has made you a bit commitment-phobic, so that you're inclined to run away from someone who treats you properly? If your ex turned up on your doorstep and begged to have you back, would you really want him? Is your new man really less romantic, sexually adept and exciting than your ex? Does he really have exactly the same faults as your old man, only magnified? The answer to all the above could well be 'yes' but it could equally easily be your emotions playing tricks on you – they have a tendency to do that. One thing's for sure though: unless you can nip any negative behaviour in the bud and enjoy the new relationship you're in without harking back to your ex, it makes a lot more sense to split up with your new man. Spend some time single so that you can sort your head out and get yourself ready to be in a relationship, without carting a load of baggage around with you.

If the idea of splitting up with your man breaks your heart, even though you still have some residual issues to deal with about your ex, get thee to a relationship counsellor (alone, at least to start with). You may find that a bit of therapy will help you move on from your ex and enjoy your new relationship without any horrors resurfacing from the past. The one thing you shouldn't do is just ignore any rumblings and hope they'll go away. Much as time is a healer, if you're going through a tough time getting over your ex while dating someone else, chances are you'll take it out on the new man, and that's just not fair.

As you can see, exes aren't exactly easy to deal with when you're in a relationship. There are numerous problems that your exes can cause for you. But if you sit down, work your way through those problems and solve them, then you're on your way to a perfect relationship. All you need to worry about then is being a good ex to everyone you've ever dated, so that you can share the joy.

Ten things never to tell a man about your ex

1. You're still in love with him.
2. He used to be a porn star but he gave it up because he got fed up of the women in the industry complaining he was too big to work with. You've got the videos to prove it if he wants to see them...
3. He has a penis smaller than a maggot (new man will assume you're lying – and worry about what you'll say about him should you ever split up).
4. He's buried in the back garden because he accused you of having PMT when it was perfectly obvious to anyone that you were absolutely fine, actually.
5. He's the only man to have ever given you an orgasm (particularly if you've already started getting it on with the new guy).

6. He's insanely jealous and would beat up anyone who so much as looked at you.

7. He's an Olympic-level athlete who races sports cars in his spare time (if he was, lie and say you never asked him about what he did for a living).

8. He's the only man who could ever have persuaded you to try all the deviant sexual things you ended up exploring together and you could never, ever do them again.

9. He's so rich that Bill Gates calls him up when he needs a loan.

10. He's your new man's dad — and you now know for sure that penis size is hereditary.

Chapter 5

Being a Good Ex

After all that lot, you'd think that your ex-iquette would be about as polished as it could possibly be, but you'd be wrong. There's still the small matter of being a good ex to worry about. After all, if you expect your exes to be nice to you, and your partner's exes to behave in a proper manner towards him, then it's only fair that you share the joy by being a flawless ex yourself.

When it comes to being the perfect ex, a lot of it depends on the person you're the ex to. Some guys prefer it if their previous partners vanish into the ether, never to be heard from again. Others like staying friends with their exes, in which case just follow the advice in Chapter 2 (assuming that you want to become friends with him), while still others love having their exes simmering away on the back-burner as a potential harem, should times get hard action-wise.

It doesn't take a genius to work out which category your ex fits into. If he keeps every conversation brief when you call him and never wants to meet up with you, then you're stalking the poor man, and he really doesn't want to retain any kind of relationship with you. Let go. Harassing someone isn't going to change their mind and make them magically turn round and declare their undying love. It'll just drag your self-esteem further into the toilet, which isn't what you need. Delete your ex's number, stop going to the places that you know he'll be and focus on enjoying your life now rather than trying to live in the past. There's nothing that you can do to make someone fall in love with you, and no matter how unfair or heartbreaking it may seem, the only thing you can do is move on.

If your ex calls you up, or happily chats away when you call him and still hangs out with you on occasion, it's cool and groovy to stay in contact — just make sure that neither of you is operating under false illusions and actually wants to have a relationship. Who knows, you could have the basis of a beautiful friendship.

And if your ex calls you but only ever at 11 pm (or whenever the clubs have closed) then he's interested in one thing, and one thing alone. Unless you make the best cup of coffee or cheese on toast on the planet, you know what it is. It's entirely up to you whether you want to keep your ex as a fuck buddy but, with this kind of behaviour, he's not exactly behaving like a buddy most of the time so all you'll really be getting is fucked.

Harriet's story: I thought I was using him, but I ended up feeling used

When Richard and I split up, we fell into the habit of having sex every few weeks or so. He'd call me and beg me for it, which made me feel great, because I felt like I still had power over him even though we were no longer a couple. I guess a part of me figured that he couldn't resist me because I'm so sexy, which made me feel good about myself – he always gave me compliments about my body so it seemed to fit. More to the point, the sex with him had never been the problem between us so it felt like I'd got the best of both worlds: none of the annoyance of dating him, but still having someone who knew what they were doing to regularly have sex with.

Then one night I was feeling frisky so I gave him a call. He was really short with me and said that he was busy before hanging up so promptly that it almost felt like he'd slammed the phone down on me. I realised that the arrangement only went one way: he was just using me for sex whenever he failed to pull. I was the one being used, not him.

I cried myself to sleep that night and from then on, ignored his calls, even though it was hard. Luckily, I met a new guy about a month ago and I feel much better about myself now – I'd never put up with that sort of treatment again.

As Harriet's story shows, being a good ex isn't just about making your old partner feel comfortable and doing what he wants. You also need to do the right thing for yourself. There's no point staying friends with an ex that you find as interesting as grouting the bathroom or having sex with an ex because you feel that you should rather than because you want to. That doesn't make you a good ex: it makes you a sucker, with possible martyr tendencies.

As a general rule, the best thing to do is to be yourself and do what feels natural. However, if strong emotions are involved then sometimes you need to moderate your behaviour, and, ideally, try to resolve any negativity that still remains so that you can move on. For example, if someone dumps you and you can't understand why, it's perfectly acceptable for you to try to get to the bottom of what happened, for the sake of your own sanity. However, you can't guarantee your ex will be willing to talk to you – or expect them to. As such, the moderate way to behave is to ask your ex if you can see them one last time to sort your head out, or, failing that, write them a letter laying out your feelings (trying hard to be as unemotional as possible – this isn't about playing the blame-game; it's about clearing out any manky feelings so you can get rid of any associated baggage).

Do make sure that when you ask to see someone to get closure, you aren't just using it as an excuse to see your ex one more time. Ask the questions that you need answered, get them resolved, thank your ex for his time and then pack that relationship up into a bundle marked 'history' and set off towards your future. If your partner refuses to meet up with you to give you closure, sorry, but you have to accept that it's their decision. You'll need to resolve your feelings on your own — you can always see a professional counsellor if you find getting over your ex as hard as wallowing through treacle while carrying a wasp's nest in each hand.

Some women get aggressive or vindictive after the break-up of a relationship and end up trying to seek revenge on their ex, either directly by slashing their tyres, or indirectly by making their lives hell with endless phone calls and passive-aggressive conversations. This is obviously not 'good ex' behaviour. Exactly what purpose does it really serve to call your ex repeatedly at 2 am demanding answers, or to return all the presents he bought for you, chopped up into tiny pieces? There's no fun in being a bunny boiler (well, not much) and it certainly won't make you appealing to any other men, so check that you don't make any of the following mistakes:

- *Sending more than two text messages or leaving more than two phone messages for an ex in a row, without getting a reply from him.* If he doesn't reply after two attempts to initiate contact, he doesn't want to talk to you. Either that or he's busy and he'll get back to you when he has the time and inclination. Harsh as it is, you need to accept this. Imagine your ex as a bar of wet soap — the more pressure you apply, the further away he's likely to slip.
- *Obsessing over a petty item that you've left at your ex's place — say, a pair of knickers — and turning up at his house late at night or first thing in the morning, unprompted, so that you can get it back.* Then 'accidentally' forgetting to take it with you so that you can repeat the whole cycle again.

Or worse, slipping them into his bed so that any other women he pulls will find them and think he's bad news.

- *Spreading negative rumours about your ex.* Particularly in places where you know he's likely to try to pull.
- *Returning gifts that he bought you, whether intact or broken.* Any presents you were given during the course of a relationship are yours. Giving them back is a hurtful way to try to show you're rejecting your ex as much as they rejected you. It's petty and cruel – he probably put thought into the gifts, and meant them at the time. If that's not enough to put you off, think about it – if you return the presents he could give them to another woman. And you probably wouldn't like *that* very much at all.

Assuming that you manage to bypass negative actions, and pay attention to your ex's behaviour so that you respond accordingly to what he wants (bearing in mind what you want too) then you'll probably be a good ex. However, there are a few traps that you might fall into, particularly if you stay single for a while after the pair of you split.

Being a good ex while you're single

If you've stayed friends with your ex then just follow all the rules about that detailed in Chapter 2 and you won't go far wrong. It's when you're not mates with your ex that you need to be careful as a single woman. It's all too easy to find yourself calling your ex three glasses of wine down. Drunken dialling is never a good idea. The conversations you think you're having rarely reflect your actual words, which can only lead to trouble. For example, here's a conversation you may think you're having when drunk:

You: Hope all's going well. I was just calling to say that I'd like the money back that you lent me.

Him: Yeah, fine, I'm paid tomorrow. How's you?

You: I'm great. I've got a new man, actually. He's nice. I mean, not as much of a charmer as you, but it's good. Anyway, meet you at lunchtime at your work to get the cash?

Him: Sure, see you then.

Using the wonders of alcohol-translation, it will transpire that you've actually had one of the following conversations, when you wake up feeling hung-over and guilty in the morning, check your mobile phone log, see that you called your ex and have to call him again to find out why you called him in the first place.

You: Oi, you bastard. When am I going to get my money back? You're such a thieving git. I hope you're having a really nice life right now, just like you deserve.

Him: [Sarcastically] Great to here from you too. I told you you'll get your money. I get paid tomorrow so I'll sort it out then.

You: At long bloody last. I need it urgently, you know, because I've got a new man who's much better than you are and he's taking me on holiday somewhere really expensive so I need my spending money. He's so much more generous than you were. And he's got a much bigger cock. I don't know what I ever saw in you. Anyway, when are you going to give me my money.

Him: I've already told you, tomorrow. Let's speak then when you've sobered up.

or

You: Hi gorgeous, I was wondering, you know that money, can I get it back from you now? Just pop round your house and, you know, get it ... Assuming you're feeling perky...

Him: Yeah, I'm fine, err, bit busy right now.

You: I wish I was getting busy right now. OK, I've got that new guy but he's nothing compared to you, if you know what I mean. So, shall I ... come ... over?

Him: Err, let's see each other at lunchtime tomorrow. Bye.

Of course the latter case may well alternatively lead to sex with the ex but if you're calling him drunk, it's a fairly safe bet that this isn't a man that you should be having sex with, or at least that you haven't thought things through properly. The pussy is no better at making intelligent decisions than the cock.

To avoid drunken dialling, change the pin that locks your phone to a really long number. That way you won't be able to remember it when you're drunk. Alternatively, ask a friend to confiscate your phone until you get home (at which point, if you're still hammered, she should take your phone battery home with her). Or just use your willpower. Otherwise you'll only regret it in the morning.

It's not just drunken dialling that can make you a bad ex by being overly aggressive or demanding. Desperation can be as powerful an intoxicant as alcohol. And so it is that you may find yourself scrolling through your phone book and calling your exes for a chat, particularly when you've got PMT, then rapidly descending into either demands for sex or sobbing pleas that they tell you what's wrong with you and why you weren't good enough for them. Unless an ex is a friend, don't do it: delete their number (if they are a friend, still don't do it but you can keep their number in your phone). Otherwise you're giving yourself ammunition that will backfire on you and make you look needy if you use it. Sure, it's nice getting ego-boosts from men but your exes are not the people to turn to. If you dumped them then it'll just lead them on and hurt them unfairly. And if they dumped you then it'll make you seem like a clingy nightmare.

The way that you behave when you see an ex (who you're not friends with) is also important. Unless they really destroyed you deliberately and maliciously – and it's a rare man that does this – the best way to handle it is with grace. Smile sweetly, nod hello and move on. Don't try to get chatting with them – it's too easy to end up having a defensive conversation and over-justifying how happy and 'over them' you are. Showing that you can be polite makes you the better woman (and there's a reasonable chance that it'll really bug them, particularly if they're with a new girlfriend when you see them).

The main rule with exes is, if they're friends, behave as a friend. If they're not, forget all about them because they're no longer a relevant part of your life. They're a 'once upon a time', not a 'happily ever after'.

Being a good ex when you're attached

When you're dating someone else, it's often easier to cope with your exes. You're less likely to feel lonely and decide that you need to call an ex for reassurance (or sex). However, you may still find yourself thinking about your ex, or comparing your new man to the old one. This is where you need to be careful if you bump into your ex. It can be tempting to brag about how fantastic your new partner is; how they know you so much better, take more care of you, turn you on and are an all-round improvement on your ex.

Sometimes this is loved-up keenness and at other times it's a more manipulative attempt to belittle your ex (often particularly tempting if they're the one that dumped you). Either way, it's best avoided. Boasting about how fabulous your new man is just looks petty and desperate, as if you haven't moved on (probably because you haven't). Added to which, it's likely to bruise your ex's ego and possibly hurt him – and hurting other people just isn't nice behaviour. Just be content that you've found someone new, and release your ex from your mind.

Rave to your mates about your new man, not your exes, and act with class towards anyone who was unfortunate enough not to keep hold of a relationship with you. That way you'll be behaving in an ex-emplary fashion.

Coping with your ex's new partner

Regardless of whether you're single or attached, the hardest thing of all can often be coping with an ex's new partner. If you're not friends with your ex, this is easily dealt with. Just smile sweetly, be polite and move on if you bump into your man with his ex, as detailed above. But if you're friends, the whole issue can be a lot more complicated.

Like it or not, and regardless of who finished the relationship, the second your ex gets a new partner, you're likely to end up comparing yourself to her – and generally find that your self-esteem suffers as a result. If she is, in your opinion, more attractive than you are then you may find yourself wishing that you were thinner, or had bigger breasts, or had longer hair because she has and it makes you feel bad about the way you look. And if she's less attractive than you are then you may find yourself querying your personality – if she's that unattractive then how could anyone possibly choose her over you?

Janine's story: She was so rough

When I broke up with my fiancé, Sam, it was a mutual decision. Things hadn't been right for a while and deep down I knew we wouldn't have lasted together forever. But it still hurt when he got engaged less than a year after we split up. We'd been together for ten years and it had taken him eight to propose to me. I felt like I'd been demoted. And when I saw a picture of her I was disgusted. She was mousy, fat and flat-chested and had a pallid complexion. She looked a lot older than me and had terrible fashion sense. I couldn't believe I'd been passed over for her. It made me feel as if I was uglier than her, even though I knew that in reality I was much prettier.

Then I started to worry about what it said about my personality. For my ex to date that monster, she had to have a really good personality. But when I eventually met her at a party held by mutual friends of mine and Sam's, a brief embarrassing conversation suggested she didn't. Then I thought it must be down to her bedroom antics, but I've always been confident about my skills and I couldn't see how she could be that much better than me.

It was only a few years later that I realised the truth. Sam was talking about her and he was obviously still smitten, even though, by now, they'd been married for a while. She was simply the right woman for him, and her looks and personality were irrelevant. It wasn't a comparison between me and her. He just loved her more. It hurt, but in a way it made me feel better, because I knew there was nothing that I could have done differently to change the way things panned out.

This is normal human insecurity and, as such, should be firmly put back into its place as a negative emotion that's only going to cause you pain. It doesn't benefit anyone so why bother humouring it?

If you don't tackle your self-esteem issues, you may find yourself bitching and sniping at your ex, or find yourself feeling as rejected as you did when you first split up, no matter how much time has passed. You need to realise that your ex's dating habits are not a reflection on you. He went out with you. It didn't work for whatever reasons. He's dating someone else now. End of story. He's not trying to replace you, better you or belittle you (at least not unless he's a really messed-up puppy). He's just trying to get on with his life and you should follow his lead.

Carrie's story: I thought I was fine but I was wrong

After Craig and I split up, we tried to stay friends, though I did find it hard because, in all honesty, I was still in love with him. It didn't help that he started dating someone new within a week of us splitting up, which felt like a betrayal of everything we'd ever had. I hated her, hated him, felt that his behaviour showed how unimportant I was to him and generally felt destroyed. We tried to stay friends because we genuinely liked each other but I often got irritable with him when her name cropped up because it made me feel bad about myself. I couldn't understand how he could move on so quickly. Nonetheless, having him as a friend was better than not having him at all.

We did bicker quite a lot to start with because I couldn't let go of the past and got jealous every time he mentioned his new (thinner than me, younger than me, more stylish than me) girlfriend. But over time, we worked through all our demons and, even though I didn't date anyone else, once I'd had a couple of casual rendezvous I started to feel better. At the same, when he split up with the 'better than me' woman, I found it a lot easier to be his friend. He was fairly messed up about it and chose me to confide in. There were nights when I went home and cried because of the way that he said he'd felt about her and the details he shared with me but it felt worth it to have that intimacy with him,

At around this time, he also lost his job. He's always been passionate about his career – it was one of the things that I found sexy about him – so he was absolutely destroyed. I was the person that he turned to for help and, through the late-night confessions and occasional (manly) tears, our friendship moved on from me hoping he'd realise how brilliant I am and ask me to go back out with him to proper best-friendship. As I got to know him better, I realised how incompatible we were: he's selfish (and proud of it) and is attracted to similarly selfish people; I love buying friends small presents, being a good hostess and helping anyone I can. He's naturally messy; I'm a clean freak. There were a million tiny reasons that we were wrong for each other and over a period of months our friendship developed. Part of me was worried that I'd be jealous again if he started dating anyone else though – I still had a huge crush on him.

But when he told me about other women he'd slept with, it didn't really upset me that much.

Then one day he called to tell me his ex wanted to see him to 'get closure'. He asked my advice and, much as I hated the idea, I encouraged him to see her because it was important for his state of mind that he got things cleared up with her. They ended up having sex. I guessed what was going on before it happened – he said nothing would happen but I know him well enough to know what he's like. When he begrudgingly admitted to it the morning after, I felt terrible. Suddenly all my old negative feelings came back. He liked her better than me, she was prettier than me, I was worthless – a whole host of nasty thoughts floating around my brain. I honestly felt that if I could wipe her off the face of the planet – not kill her but just some-how make it so that she'd never existed – then I'd be a happier person.

I kept the feelings in for a while but eventually I had to confess to Craig why my behaviour had changed so much: I'd become insecure, needy and full of self-loathing – all very unattractive. Once he realised what was going on, he promised not to mention her to me again, at least in any detail. I hated that she existed but could cope with it, as long as I didn't have to deal with hearing about how great she smelled, how good the chemistry was and how right it felt when he was with her. It's odd because I'm not jealous of other women he's with but because she was the ex that replaced me, I guess I'll always see her as competition.

Sadly, such is the power of emotions that there's a risk you may decide you want your ex back now that someone else has got him, even though the mere idea would have been a turn-off the week before – and even if you already have a new partner. This is immature 'dog in the manger' behaviour that you should do your best to ignore. Sure, there's a slim chance that your ex really was 'the one' and it's taken you until now to realise it but it's a lot more likely that your ego is yelping because now you've been 'replaced' and it doesn't like it. Ride the feeling through, think about your ex's negative attributes and above all, don't contact your ex to share your feelings for at least a month. You'll probably find, after the initial stinging, that you're far happier now that your ex has got a new partner because it makes things less complicated when you go out for an evening. And it'll certainly make your new man feel more comfortable about you spending time with your ex.

And if the feelings do continue? Think carefully before fronting up to them. OK, there's a chance that you might get back together and live happily ever after, but it's a lot more likely that you'll end up ruining any relationship that you have with your ex, making things uncomfortable for everyone. You need to be aware that admitting your feelings may mean that you end up having no contact at all with your ex – and that may well be for the best.

The new girl

And then there's how to cope with the new girlfriend herself. If you're not friends with your ex then it's not that likely that you'll run into each other very often, so there's not too much to worry about. Just make sure that you don't slag your man off if you do run into him with his new girlfriend, and don't assume his new girlfriend is an evil bitch because she's 'got your man' – she hasn't, she's got your ex. It's all too easy to take your aggression out on the woman who's now dating your ex when she's actually done nothing other than have the same taste in men as you.

If, on the other hand, you're friends with your ex, you may find yourself going too far the other way in an attempt to prove that you're over him and fine with him dating someone else (it *is* OK to feel a bit of a sting when your ex starts dating someone new so you don't need to bend over backwards to pretend that you don't). Avoid making the mistake of being overly friendly and insisting on meeting his partner the second they start dating. Give her time to get to know your ex on her own, and establish her own relationship with him, unbiased by your viewpoint. Once you meet, no matter how hard you try, she'll be affected by your opinion of her man – not to mention as jealous and insecure about you as you are about her, if not more so.

Instead, wait for her to ask for contact. It's not your right to meet your ex's new partner, and unless it's something she feels a need to do, you may have to content yourself with remaining in the dark. If she does ask her man whether she can meet you, agree, and then put your emotions in check. You don't want to do anything to damage his new relationship (well, a part of you might want to but that's naughty and should be ignored).

The Ex Factor

When it comes to getting ready, make a point of dressing in a non-threatening way – now isn't the time to pull out your foxiest outfit. Don't obviously dress down though – you don't want to plunge your ex into shock at your new look or make his new woman assume that you're a nun. Just go for a standard 'first date'-style outfit – flattering without trying too hard, a bit of make-up but not the full-on night-out slap.

When it comes to talking to her, respond to your man's ex as a potential new friend rather than competition. That ship has sailed for you and now it's her turn to try to steer it. Don't pepper your conversation with mentions of your ex, or things that you've done together, and don't allow him to become the topic of conversation because he's your natural common ground. Otherwise you're only going to end up in trouble, and quite possibly with both of you in tears.

Stick to light conversation, let your ex steer it if need be – he'll know any sensitive areas much better than you do. Even better, if you have a partner, take him along with you so that there isn't an awkward gooseberry feeling, and your ex's partner can see that you're no threat because you're perfectly happy with someone else now. OK, it won't be the most fun night you've ever had but at least at the end of the night, you and your man can indulge in a bonding bitchy conversation about how dull both your ex and his new girlfriend are compared to the pair of you. OK, it's not mature but it is human.

Of course, things might go swimmingly and you could find yourself adoring your ex's new partner.

However, befriending the girlfriend is a scary tightrope walk. You need to be friendly enough that your ex feels comfortable mentioning her or taking her out to parties you're going to be at, but not so friendly that he panics you'll tell her all his dirty secrets. Remember, you were friends with your ex before his new woman came along – and if they split up, you don't want to put yourself in the awkward situation of having to choose between them. Only seriously buddy up with an ex's girlfriend if you know there's a potential for you to be better friends with her than you are with him, and that you'd be happy to lose him in favour of her. Don't expect your ex to be happy with the friendship though – and do analyse your motives about why you want such a tight friendship with an ex's partner. Are you sure it's not just a way to stay close to your ex, or keep him under control in an indirect way?

When to walk away

Whether it's by befriending an ex, befriending his new girlfriend or simply changing the pub you go to his local, it can be easy to fall into the trap of trying anything to stay close to your ex, but this isn't generally healthy. Sometimes the best place for your ex in your life is a long, long way away from you – physically and emotionally.

As a result, there are times when being a good ex is about ceasing all contact. This could be for numerous reasons. Perhaps your ex is still fixated by you and staying in contact with him means that he can't get over his feelings (even if it does keep your ego nicely stoked). Maybe you're not over him and he's freaked out by your occasional lapses into puppy dog eyes when you've had one too many drinks. Or perhaps staying friends with your ex is preventing you from moving on and forming a relationship with anyone new. While it's not necessarily healthy to leap immediately from one relationship to another, it can be cause for concern if you split with an ex then spend so much time with him 'as friends' that you're still single a year or more later.

Luisa's story: It took time but we got there

I'd been separated from Nathan and friends with him for two years when he told me that he was getting married. I hadn't dated anyone since him, at least not seriously, so he was still the last person I'd been in love with. I kind of had him 'in reserve' in case no-one else wanted me.

His marriage was the result of a whirlwind romance so I hadn't had a chance to get used to him even dating anyone else. If you'd have asked me before he told me, I'd have thought I would have been quite upset about an announcement like that. In reality, there was a minor pang but nothing fiercer. That was the point that I realised we were real friends.

Now, I feel truly free to move on and start dating other people – I didn't want to when he was still available because it didn't seem fair. I wouldn't exactly want to spend an evening with him and his wife right now, but one day I'm sure I will.

Alternatively, your ex might have a girlfriend who feels incredibly threatened by him staying friends with you but could be the love of his life if you weren't around. Or it could simply be that you don't have enough in common to be mates and he's only staying in contact with you out of politeness, or because he feels guilty about hurting you.

Walking away from an ex isn't about making dramatic pronouncements such as, 'I'm never going to see you again.' That kind of behaviour is about grabbing attention and is the antithesis of being the perfect ex. Instead, you should just cease contact with your ex, be polite but brief if he contacts you and say that you're 'busy' should he phone you up and ask to see you. Let yourself drift away from your ex, making it seem as accidental as possible, so that you're both free to move on with your own lives.

Steph's story: He's out of bounds

My ex slept with a very good friend of mine during a particularly debauched weekend, and it was extremely traumatic and horrible for me – only made worse when they started dating. Even though we'd all been friends for years, I understandably didn't want either of them in my life any more. Two years down the line it's all fine – all three of us are friends again, with the proviso that, since he's nothing but trouble, me and my friend both keep our distance. I've stuck to this promise, except for one particularly drunken weekend, when I left her in a pub somewhere and went home to have sex with him. Ha! Well, come on, nobody's perfect.

The main way to be a perfect ex is to have respect: for yourself, your ex and any new partners that may come along for either of you. If you manage that, you've almost got your ex-iquette honed to perfection.

Ten ways to be the perfect ex

1. Never mention anything negative from your previous relationship history, either to him or someone else.
2. Don't get nostalgic over 'what might have been'.
3. Listen to him when he needs someone to talk to without dragging the conversation back to what he was like when the pair of you were dating.
4. Don't tread on eggshells for fear of saying something wrong – just be yourself.
5. Be nice to any new girlfriends he gets, without being creepily over-familiar and telling them what he really likes in the bedroom.
6. Don't parade endless new men in front of him…
7. …but do tell him if you start dating anyone, particularly if it's serious.

8. Only have sex with him if you're both single and sure that it won't damage the friendship.
9. If staying in contact is messing up his life, or yours, don't be afraid to walk away.
10. Generally treat him the way that you'd like him to treat you.

Chapter 6

Chapter 6

And the Rest...

Once you've got all that lot sorted, well done – you can consider yourself an ex-pert. But there are still a few special little treats that you might have to deal with in certain situations. Conflict can arise when you meet your new man's friends; his ex-wife; his kids. Or you might even find yourself having to deal with his ex-boyfriend. All of these situations are perfectly easy to deal with (though in the case of the latter, it's probably best to walk away if you also find out that you've dated the same ex, and neither of you are over him, unless you've got an extremely dark sense of humour).

For example, if a man's relatively freshly out of a long-term relationship, it's pretty likely that his friends will know his ex. Some of them may even still maintain a friendship with her. As such you could find yourself facing hostility when you meet them, particularly from any female friends (men tend to be more no-bullshit about these sort of things and just get one with it –

either that or they can be bribed with a few pints).

The best way to deal with this is with time and grace. Don't rush to buddy up with your man's best mates. If they were – or are still – friends with his ex, they may feel disloyal so they'll need time to get over that concern. Taking your time means that they'll get to know the real you rather than seeing you merely as 'the ex replacement'. And with any luck they'll like you – as long as you're just yourself. Added to which, if you try too hard to impress your partner's friends, they'll sense your desperation and they won't warm to you, which could cause problems in your relationship.

Lorna's story: I competed with her even though I didn't need to

When I met Alastair, I was over the moon. It was love at first sight – seemingly for both of us – and I really thought I'd found 'the one'. He was well-read, incredibly bright, funny, gorgeous, and could do things to my body that made it feel better even than I could. There was only one problem: his ex, Janey. I'd never met her but from everything he'd told me – which was a fair bit – she was every bit as intelligent as he was, naturally beautiful, innately stylish and at ease in any social situation. I was haunted by her ghost. When we were on our own, I managed to forget about her – after all, he was with me now – but when he invited me to a party with a large group of their mutual friends, I was petrified.

And the Rest . . .

I knew that there were going to be lots of people at the party who'd known Janey – including Alastair's best friend, Sammi. Worse, I was so busy worrying about what his friends would think of me that I got distracted and forgot to pack the dress that I'd planned to wear.

I arrived at his place on the Saturday night and it wasn't until about 1 am when he mentioned the party the following afternoon that I realised I hadn't got anything to wear.

I freaked out – all I had with me was a casual micro-miniskirt and a T-shirt top because it was the middle of summer. I was so worried that Alastair's friends would think I was some flighty young airhead that I insisted we went shopping the next morning, before the party, for a new outfit.

It was hell. The shops were too hot, nothing fitted and when I got home and tried on the outfit I'd hurriedly bought in desperation, it looked all wrong. I was almost in tears in front of the mirror.

When I arrived at the party I was distracted. Sammi very sweetly complimented me on my outfit but I knew that I looked all wrong. As a result, I laughed too hard, and wouldn't wander far from Alastair's side because I felt intimidated and was concerned about not fitting in. It was a disaster. His friends were very lovely but I couldn't let them see the real me.

That night Alastair and I had a huge row that, in hindsight, was the beginning of the end. I'd been so threatened by the idea of his ex that I'd tried to be her

– and in doing so, forgotten to be myself. That was what Alastair had loved, so why did I want to be a pale imitation of Janey?

I realised, once I'd worked things through after our break-up, that if I wanted a successful relationship in future I'd need to remember not to compete with another woman – real or imagined – ever again.

Generally speaking, a man's friends just want him to be happy so once they see that you're making him that way, they'll like you because you have a positive effect on their mate.

The same principles can be applied to dealing with your new man's family if they're hung up on the ex. The best way to avoid conflict is by not rushing into meeting them. Leave it for a few months before you do the parent thing. That way they have time to get used to the idea that their beloved son has left the woman they wanted him to marry. It also has fringe benefits: once you've met a man's parents, it's likely you'll get yourself invited back and feel obliged to go, so you're saving yourself endless dull weekends by delaying the inevitable (assuming the relationship lasts).

When you do finally meet your man's parents, be polite, take a bunch of flowers or some wine, don't rise to any negative statements they might make, ignore any pictures of the ex around the place and give the relationship time to develop. Accept yourself and your man's parents will be more likely to accept you. If they don't, at least you've handled the situation with grace.

'Til death us do part – but she didn't die

Given the world that we live in, it might not just be his friends and family that cause problems. Nowadays, a third of all marriages end in divorce so when you meet a single guy, there's a reasonable risk that he'll have an ex-wife loitering in the background, particularly as you get older. You might get lucky – the marriage could have ended long ago, and amicably. Then again, you might not live in a fairy-tale world and the ex could be still arguing about signing the divorce papers or, worse, living in the house with your partner because they haven't been able to sell it and neither of them can afford to move out.

If that's the case, be understanding but with limits. Ask what their ground-rules are – did they agree that neither would have anyone stay over, for example – and don't be scared to set a few of your own. Perhaps you can go to see your man's flat when his ex is at work or stay over when she's away. Maybe you want him to stop wandering round in a bath towel in front of her. Or perhaps you're happy to accept them living together as long as it's for no more than the next year. The rules depend on the relationship they have and the situation you're dealing with. However, you can guarantee that neither of them are finding the situation ideal either, so it's better to be understanding and bide your time until they stop living together. Rowing about it with your man or leaving property papers with flats circled in it for his ex won't have any positive effect – in fact, quite the opposite.

When your man's ex finally does move out (or vice versa) don't insist on having a big celebration. There's a reasonable chance your man might feel down, not because he wants to be with her but because it's the end of an era. Let him have his space and decide what he wants to do. After all, he's only just got back to having a place all to himself again, and that's a big step.

The same goes if a guy's getting divorced. You might want to scream 'hallelujah!' from the rooftops but it's entirely understandable if he gets a bit nostalgic. He stood at an altar (or beach, or registry office) and said he'd love his ex-wife forever. It's hardly surprising if he has a brief pang of regret when the final chapter closes on their relationship.

Tori's story: She saw more of him than I did

I met Darren at a party and copped off with him that night. He was so cute that I couldn't resist. We went for lunch together the next day, he asked me on a date for the day after and within a couple of weeks we were boyfriend and girlfriend. It all happened so quickly that I didn't really have time to think about things that much. Darren mentioned that he was in the process of getting divorced but it seemed too soon for me to pry for the details.

Then I called him up to rearrange a date as I had to work late, and a woman answered the phone. I hadn't talked about his living arrangements with him but I assumed it must be his flatmate. She passed me over to him and I asked who it was. I was utterly shocked when he told me it was his wife.

That night over dinner he explained things to me properly. Apparently, the flat they'd bought together was still on the market. It was their first flat and they couldn't afford to sell it for less than the asking price because they'd only owned it for a year and were already going to lose money. They'd spent every penny on moving and neither of them could afford to rent anywhere else, so they had to live together until the flat was sold. He was keen to reassure me that they had separate rooms and lived independently.

I really didn't like the idea of Darren living with his ex-wife but what could I do? We'd only been together for a matter of weeks so it was way too soon for me to ask him to move in with me. If I wanted to be with him, I had to grin and bear it.

And so I did. It made things a bit tricky – I couldn't stay over at his place unless his wife was away because it felt wrong. And occasionally I'd get jealous thinking that he might see her when she'd just got out the shower, or she might see him drunk and take advantage. But Darren kept on reassuring me and, for the most part, it was OK. I even met her a few times and although we'd never be best of mates, she was nice enough. I could see she didn't want to be with Darren any more than he wanted to be with her.

I'm glad I held in there. The flat finally sold after a year, and Darren and I were still together. That was three years ago. Now, we've got a place of our own together, and we plan to get married in the summer. It was a weird situation at first but it was worth the wait.

Coping with your man's kids

Having an ex-wife to deal with can be bad enough, but if your man has kids from a previous relationship then you've got even more on your plate. If they're adult children then just deal with them as you would a man's friends, albeit more sensitively. But if they're still young enough to live at home, be prepared for more of a struggle. It's all very well complaining about a man's ex being controlling, after all, but saying the same thing about his 'sweet and innocent' monsters is something else entirely. And there's also a big difference between an ex and 'the mother of his children'.

First things first: a man's kids aren't a stand-alone thing. They usually come with the mother – his ex – attached, which means that there are potentially two sets of relationships that you'll need to build. Before you can get anywhere near the kids, you need to get the mother onside. The only problem is that she probably holds all the cards: most child custody cases result in the mother holding the baby, which means she can deny access (legally or illegally) – something no decent man will want. So you have to play by her rules to stand any hope of winning.

To start with, you need to meet her. Unless she demands contact, don't insist on meeting the mother of your man's kids too early — but do make sure that you meet her before you meet them. Otherwise, she's likely to feel resentful and threatened that you're trying to take over her role. Chances are she'll feel bad enough that you're moving in on her ex (it's just normal jealousy, she's not a psycho. Remember, in biological terms, this is the father of her children that you're dating, so it's understandable if she gets a bit 'lioness' on you). The last thing you want is for her to think that you're trying to steal her kids too — have you ever seen a lioness when her cubs are threatened?

Be on your best behaviour when you meet her, no matter how bitchy she is to you: remember, your man split with her and is now seeing you so, whether she wants him or not, she'll be feeling hurt, and when a mammal's in pain it lashes out. Keep the first meeting brief — a coffee or quick drink together before she drops the kids off with your man. All she needs to know about you is that you're a vaguely responsible human being, aren't trying to be 'mummy' and don't have a drug habit/alcohol problem/anything else that's likely to make you unsafe for her kids to be around. You don't need to become best buddies but, like it or not, if your man has kids then their mum is part of your life.

Be calm and friendly when you see her and accede to any reasonable demands that she makes and with any luck, things should be fine. If she starts making unreasonable demands, you need to talk about it with your man, calmly and without her present, and decide whether there are compromises that you're willing to make for the sense of harmony or if she's asking you to go several steps too far. If your ex refuses to step in and help matters at all, think about whether you really want to be with someone who won't support you. If you do, this is a battle you'll have to fight alone, and you probably won't win. Remember, the mother of the child holds all the cards. Good luck.

Assuming you've got the mum side of the equation dealt with, the bigger step is meeting the kids. Don't rush into this. You certainly shouldn't meet the kids until you've been with your partner for at least three months and ideally a lot longer, so that you're sure it's a secure relationship. Children are easily hurt and you don't want to form a relationship with them too quickly only to lose them along with your man should you split up. Otherwise you won't be the only one feeling confused about what happened.

When you do meet your partner's kids, be friendly but not over-friendly. Don't try to bribe them or become their 'best mate' or (heaven forbid) a mother figure. You're their father's girlfriend, not their stepmum. You don't need to deal with all the baggage that comes with step-motherhood unless you move in with your man or get married, and that's another book entirely.

Ask your partner to keep the first meeting as short as possible, ideally with some form of distraction going on — say, a trip to the park or to the cinema, depending on their age — so you don't find yourself talking too much to fill in an awkward silence, or facing an inquisition from a surly row of kids. Making an effort is all well and good but you're dating your man not his children – they're just part of the package that you have to deal with.

That said, don't ignore your partner's kids entirely. If you're in a serious relationship then you do need to accept that his children are an important part of his life and, if he's not a complete git, they'll almost always come first. If you don't get on with them, it's more likely he'll get rid of you than them. He helped create them, and they're his responsibility: you're merely his recreation.

...or helping him cope with yours

Of course, it might not be your partner who has the kids to deal with. You might be the one that has children from a previous relationship. If so, do mention your kids relatively early on in the relationship. If you don't you're bound to end up bumping into him at the supermarket, when you're dealing with one of your kids who is having a tantrum because you won't buy them sweets; or worse, your new man might see you with your ex and your kids and leap to entirely the wrong conclusion. Hell, it happens in chick-lit all the time.

However, be similarly wary about introducing your own kids to a new man too quickly. Wait until you're sure that a relationship is serious before you take your man to meet your kids. And when you do go for it, be aware of the following tricks that your kids might pull on your new man:

- Encouraging your partner to bribe them with presents.
- Lying to your partner about things that you like and dislike.
- Feigning illness when you have a date arranged.
- Telling your ex about your partner after they've met.
- Telling your ex total lies about your partner after they've met.
- Constantly talking about how great daddy is whenever your new man's in the room.
- Screaming, 'You're not my daddy,' the second your partner asks them to do anything, however reasonable.
- Transferring all their affection from your ex to your partner.

Bear in mind that your kids are only doing this because they're feeling insecure and unsure about their own lives. That doesn't make it forgivable but have a quiet word with them alone rather than immediately leaping to the defence of your partner. Otherwise your children might feel that you're siding with your new man over them, which will only make them harder to deal with.

There's also another reason to be wary about introducing new partners to your kids until you're sure you know them well. You need to protect your kids: they are massively important, after all.

Lily's story: He took his resentment out on my daughter

When I met Scott I was just out of an unhappy marriage. I was looking for comfort and he was more than willing to provide it, even though I had a two-year-old daughter. He got on well with Jenny and was just as happy spending family time with the pair of us as time alone with me. He even taught her how to read.

We got married nine months after we met but the cracks soon started to show. He was jealous about my ex because he'd 'got there first' and started drinking to cope with his jealousy. Soon, he was coming home from the pub so drunk on Friday nights that I had to lock me and Jenny in the bathroom so that he wouldn't hit us.

Things came to a head when I walked in to find him slapping Jenny in the face after she'd accidentally hit him with her conker during a game. She was only four. He was screaming at her and calling her the 'bastard child'. She was just standing there, white-faced and immobile, clearly not sure what to do. I ran in to get her, scooped her under my arm and we ran out the door to my mum's. I divorced him after that. I never realised that he hated my ex so much that he'd hit my child. I wish I'd got to know him a lot better before we got married – I'd be a lot happier now, and so would Jenny. She's now six but she's turned from being a bright and funny child to one that's withdrawn and nervous. It's the biggest mistake I ever made.

Of course, most situations don't get anything like as bad as Lily's. The majority of men out there are perfectly safe around kids: but if your kids are important to you then you owe it to them to suss out a new partner as carefully as you can. Make sure your new man doesn't have any resentment about your ex that he could take out on you or your kids long before you ever introduce him to them.

Dealing with the same-sex ex

It might not be kids that cause problems, but rather, some other aspect of a partner's past. In today's world of floating sexuality, there's now a risk that you might find yourself sharing an ex with your man. Perhaps you had a girlie snog at a party and, when you bump into his ex at a party, you realise that it was with her. Or maybe you introduce your man to an old male university friend and watch them both blanch.

If this does happen, the only way to deal with it is either with abject mutual denial or, more sensibly, with an honest conversation. Dealing with reality is generally less unpleasant than dealing with your own imagination, after all. It's probably best not to confess to your partner while the third party is still there though – or to quiz them if you think they're the one with the secret. Some things are best talked about in private.

Pamela's story: She was a drunken night to me – and 'the ex' to him

I wouldn't call myself a lesbian but I did have one experience with a woman about two years ago, when I first split up with a long-term ex. I guess I was looking to experiment, and I'd had a bit too much to drink, so when this pretty blonde girl asked me to kiss her at a New Year's party, I just went with it. We ended up making out on the sofa for most of the night – nothing too serious, though our hands were going everywhere – but she vanished after we'd taken a break to dance, and other than the occasional naughty memory, it wasn't a big part of my life.

Christopher, on the other hand, was. I met him after I'd come to the end of my 'wild year' as I call it, and we bonded naturally. It took a few months for us to get together – there was a lot of flirting first and both of us were too nervous to make the first move – but when we eventually did get it on, sparks flew.

Like me, Christopher had split up with his ex a couple of years before. It had been long-term but they'd both outgrown the relationship. When I saw a picture of her, I realised it was the girl from the party – or at least, I'm pretty certain it was. She looked like the girl I remember and the timing fits – she'd have just split up with Christopher and was probably doing the same thing as me. I've never told Chris about it – I don't know how to. It'd really hurt him – not to mention raise lots of questions – when it really was no big deal to me.

Look on the bright side: if you have an ex in common with your new man, it does suggest that you're quite similar to him — or at least share the same taste in attributes you're looking for in a partner. Things could be worse.

Even if you don't have that much of a coincidence to deal with, you could find yourself getting freaked out if you learn that your partner has an ex of the same gender. Relax. According to US sexpert Kinsey, nearly half the male population had experimented with another guy at some stage in their life, and that was back in the 1950s, so it's not exactly uncommon. Other than making sure that your partner's got a clean bill of sexual health and has been tested since he last had unprotected sex — which you should do with a partner regardless of their sexuality — the main thing you need to do here is get over yourself. So your partner's had same-sex experiences. Big deal. At least he's not a homophobe.

Some women worry that a partner who's had same-sex experiences is more likely to stray. Just because someone's bisexual — or experimental — it doesn't mean they're more likely to cheat. It's monogamy that's important (assuming, of course, that it is important to you), not sexuality. Your man is no more likely to leave you because he's pining after sex with men, than a straight man is to leave you because he's pining for sex with other women. OK, still not great odds but it's certainly nothing to be particularly concerned about.

Katy's story: At first I was freaked out – then I thought it was hot

I never thought for a second that Matt could be gay. He's so manly – not macho but certainly not remotely camp. So when we were out one night and a guy came up to him and kissed him hello on the cheek, I was surprised. It's not Matt's normal style at all. I asked him who the guy was and he blustered something about it being 'a friend' but I knew that something was up.

When we got home, I asked him again who the man that had kissed him was, and how he knew him. He admitted that they used to be vague friends then one night he'd drunkenly ended up letting things get 'intimate'. He said he hadn't done anything – he'd just enjoyed having his cock sucked. Apparently the other guy had been quite into him so he'd gone out for beers with him a couple more times – he was worried that if he didn't, the guy might make a scene and tell everyone what had happened. I was so shocked by his confessions. When I pushed him further he said that he'd ended up fondling the other guy on their second 'date'.

I wasn't sure what to say at first. All that I could think was 'my boyfriend is gay'. But Matt reassured me that it was a one-off and he'd never done anything like that since. He hadn't even fantasised about it before it had happened and now he'd experimented with it, he knew he wouldn't want to try it again. The more I thought about it, the hotter it seemed. I found myself picturing Matt with the guy we'd met, and although I didn't tell Matt in case it freaked him out, I thought about it the next time we had sex.

I guess I'd always thought that Matt was a straight lover and seeing that he had an experimental side turned me on. If he'd dated another guy properly, I might not feel the same way but because it was a fling, it's a hot idea.

What with his exes and yours, children, baggage, sexuality and the rest, you should now be fairly well primed to deal with pretty much any ex situation that life can throw at you. No guarantees though – it's amazing the complications that can ensue, courtesy of exes, and I'm not going to go into details of how to deal with a man who's fighting for custody of the cat with his ex; or kids that act like the twins in *The Parent Trap*; or how to cope with the ex who left you for your new man's ex; or any of the myriad complex situations that can occur when two or more people get together. You've got the basic tools and principles. Use them. Just remember to play nice.

Ten ex situations your man might have that scream 'run away, run away'

1. His most recent ex is one of your best mates...
2. ...or a member of your family.

3. He confesses his last few exes dumped him because of his excessive drinking – and you met him drunk in a pub.

4. He did a 'kiss and tell' story on one of his exes.

5. He split up with his last girlfriend because she took him to court on domestic violence charges...

6. ...or stalking charges.

7. He has a history of leaving relationships considerably richer than he started them.

8. He left his ex-girlfriend because he found out that she was pregnant...

9. ...or while she was pregnant.

10. His last three girlfriends are now in mental health institutions.

Conclusion

Conclusion

So is it worth all this hassle just to deal with exes? Can't you just dump any bloke with the remotest hint of ex issues, make drunken phone calls to anyone that's ever scorned you, scrawl insultingly-named penis pictures of the real bastards in the cubicles at your local pub and shag your jealous ex's best mate instead (ideally having pulled him in front of said ex)? Well, yes, obviously you can — but you'll probably end up feeling a lot more hurt if you go for the spurning and vengeance route, not to mention making yourself look like a bit of a tit.

Think about it: why does it hurt when you break up with someone? Working on the basis that pain is our body's way of telling us something's wrong, there's clearly some part of us that likes being attached. That makes sense — after all, we are designed to breed, and being single lessens your chances of breeding (actually, looking at the amount of single-parent teen mums out there versus happily attached women, desperately trying to have a kid, that's not necessarily the case, but still…).

As such, the logical solution to heartbreak might seem to be getting together with someone new as soon as you possibly can, to restore your chances of breeding once again. Except that people rushing into a relationship frequently choose the wrong person and end up in rebound hell. In all likelihood, your mind will have gone into 'insecure' mode thanks to the end of the relationship. And the body isn't exactly the best judge of character either. All it wants is someone reliable enough to impregnate you and protect you from predators. It doesn't give a shit about a twinkle in the eye, good sense of humour or well-stocked set of bookshelves. It doesn't actually give a shit about anything except healthy sperm (don't even *think* about listening to its demands and listing that on an online dating site unless you want to attract nutters).

And so it's on to option three: fooling your body into believing there are still baby-making chances around (whether you actually want babies or not is irrelevant here – this is your body talking at a primal level, behind your back, physically impossible as that may be). By far the easiest way to do this is by maintaining a civilised relationship with your ex for long enough to help you find someone to move on to. OK, you logically know that you're not going to get back together with your ex but you're choosing the slow and gentle option of easing yourself out of the relationship – from partner to acquaintance (and who knows, maybe eventually to friend) – rather than ripping yourself out of it in one go. There's still going to be some pain but it may well be less of a shock to the system. OK, it's not always going to be possible to take this approach, but it's certainly worth aiming for. At least that way, you'll be able to exchange the occasional smile or Christmas card with someone that you once cared about enough to exchange bodily fluids with.

And while it can be tempting to bail out at the slightest hint of ex issues from a lover, sometimes it takes time for a person to heal and it's only when someone new comes along that's worth it – namely you – that they become ready to complete the final stage of getting over their ex. Men in particular are all too good at ignoring nagging insecurities and hangovers from previous relationships when they're single: why sort your head out when you can listen to Pink Floyd on full blast if things really start to hurt? By giving a man the chance to work things through – if not *too* much of a chance – you could end up in a relationship with a (finally) emotionally mature man.

Like it or not, exes are a part of your life and his. It doesn't matter how much work you do or how hard you try to forget 'the one that got away': sometimes, everyone feels a pang of nostalgia or sheds a tear for what might have been, a long, long time ago. When this happens to you, be kind to yourself rather than beating yourself up about it. Human emotions aren't all neatly filed away as soon as they're past their sell-by date. It takes time to heal and, sometimes, the only thing that will take away those last vestiges of pain is replacing every memory of a partner with a happier one about a new partner. After all, every time you're rejected, your ego gets battered and it's only when it gets validated by someone new and fanciable coming along and saying, 'Hey, I like you,' that you'll feel quite as good as you did when you were loved up. Sadly, you can't force the pace of this – you just have to wait for it to happen (making sure you're stocked up on chocolate for those nights when the pangs hit) and trust that it really will do, at the point when you're finally ready to move on.

Conversely, your man's exes are part of his life. If you met a guy who was in his 30s and had never dated anyone before, you'd think he was a bit odd so, even if his ex is a harridan who's never off the phone to him, it could be worse: he could be a clueless virgin. You can't expect your man to forget his past any more than he should expect you to abandon yours. But what you *can* demand – of yourself and of partners – is that you don't get involved unless any exes are far enough out of the equation that they don't stop your relationship from adding up.

The whole exes business is easy enough to manage, really. Just be a good ex and, if you're lucky, you'll land a man with exes as nice as you. And if not? At least you'll be happier than the woman down the road throwing paint over her ex-boyfriend's car.

Ten reasons to be glad you've got exes

1. You've had a chance to make all those embarrassing early sex mistakes with someone that you don't have to spend the rest of your life with…
2. …and you've had a chance to hone your techniques with subsequent exes so you've got at least one move you can feel proud of.

3. You've had the opportunity to get any hints of bunny boiler out of your system, with any luck while you were still young enough to be excused. Or at least only get sent to a Juvenile Detention Centre.

4. You've got at least one or two anecdotes about previous awful partners that you can tell your mates down the pub to keep them in hysterics.

5. And one or two awful secrets about your own weak points in relationships that you'll probably never confess to any of your mates but, with any hope, will learn from.

6. You've had the chance to see a variety of penises without having to subscribe to a porn channel.

7. You've had validation that people find you attractive, interesting and generally dateable (no, you're not allowed to self-pityingly sniff, 'You mean they *did*?').

8. You've had the joy of falling for someone, whether full-on 'in love' or just 'skipping along the pavement feeling perky'. Either way, it's a damned nice feeling and some people never get it, so feel grateful.

9. You've faced rejection and dealt with it — it's character building, don't you know.

10. You've had a chance to learn from your mistakes and now you can move on to someone bigger and better.

Useful Resources

Dealing with Break-ups

So You've Been Dumped
http://www.soyouvebeendumped.com
A great website, offering you the chance to share dumping stories, and trade tips on getting over the heartbreak.

The Dick List
http://www.thedicklist.com
A US-based site listing horror stories about 'dicks' women have dated. Avoid going for a revenge kick and adding your bloke's failings to the list. Instead, read other people's horror stories to see how lucky you are.

The Samaritans
UK: 08457 90 90 90
Ireland: 1850 60 90 90
www.samaritans.org.uk
The Samaritans provide confidential emotional support for people who are experiencing feelings of distress or despair, including those which may lead to suicide. The service is open 24 hours a day.

Dealing with an Addicted Ex

Al-Anon Family Groups UK and Eire

020 7403 0888

www.alcoholics-anonymous.org

Support group for friends, family and partners of alcoholics.

Dealing with a Violent Ex or Stalker

National Domestic Violence Helpline

0808 200 0247 (24 hours)

UK-based national helpline providing access to advice and support to anyone experiencing domestic violence.

Women's Aid

0808 200 0247 (24 hours)

www.womensaid.org.uk

Domestic violence helpline. Women's Aid can also give details of refuges and the availability of refuge places throughout the UK.

Scottish Domestic Abuse Helpline

0800 027 1234 (24 hours)

www.domesticabuse.co.uk

Domestic abuse helpline, providing housing, legal and benefits advice for all parts of Scotland.

Refuge

0808 200 0247 (24 hours)

www.refuge.org.uk

Provides safe, emergency accommodation through a network of refuges throughout the UK.

About the Author

Emily Dubberley (33) studied psychology at university, specialising in sexuality and covering topics including male and female attitudes to porn as well as whether women want their fantasies to come true. After being shortlisted for the *Cosmopolitan* Journalism Scholarship and the Company Fiction Writer Award, she founded www.cliterati.co.uk in 2001: a text-based sex website for women featuring erotica, a problem page, sex news and more. It now attracts over half a million hits per month.

Emily was Founding Editor of *Scarlet*, a sex magazine for women, which launched in October 2004. She is the sex agony aunt for *Look* magazine and has written for numerous publications including *FHM, more, New Woman, Elle, Men's Health, Forum*, the *Guardian, Penthouse*, the *Star* and *Glamour*, and has had articles syndicated worldwide. She wrote the four most recent *Lovers' Guide* DVDs, edited the *Lovers' Guide* magazine and helped create http://www.loversguide.com. She also wrote for the 'Joan Rivers Position' on Channel 5.

Emily has written numerous internationally published books. *The Lovers' Guide Lovemaking Deck* (Connections) was released in February 2004. *Brief Encounters: The Women's Guide to Casual Sex* (Vision – nominated for an Erotic

Award), *Things a Woman Should Know About Seduction* (Carlton), *Sex Play* (Eddison Sadd), *Sex for Busy People* (Fireside) and *You Must Be My Best Friend... Because I Hate You* (Vision) – about friendship conflict and how to deal with it – were released in 2005. *Whip Your Life into Shape: The Dominatrix Principle, I'd Rather Be Single Than Settle* and *More Sex Play* were all released in 2006, and *The Good Fantasy Guide* is due to be released in 2007. She is currently working on various books for publication over the next year.

Emily features regularly on radio stations including LBC, London Live and Kerrang! Throughout 2006 she wrote and presented a monthly podcast show called 'Sex Talk With Emily Dubberley' for Audible.co.uk, which included erotic stories, sex advice and reviews, and subsequently produced a series of five erotica anthologies for them. She is frequently quoted as a sexpert in magazines including *Cosmopolitan, Elle* and *Company*, has been involved with TV shows for all the terrestrial channels and various satellite channels (the most amusing of which entailed presenting QVC-style advertorials for Jessica Rabbit, which ran on numerous shopping channels across cable and satellite), writes for numerous websites including iVillage.co.uk and has tested over 300 sex toys in the past two years.

Brief Encounters
The Women's Guide to Casual Sex
Emily Dubberley

You don't need to be in a relationship to have sex, and this ultimate guide to no-strings sex ensures that single doesn't have to mean celibate. From pulling your ultimate lust object to getting rid of them the morning after, sex writer Emily Dubberley tells you everything you need to know to have good casual sex.

Learn how to find the kind of person you want to get naked with and what to do once the clothes come off so that you have the best sex ever. Find out how to cope with problems like lousy kissers, miniscule (and massive) members and the old nightmare of working out someone's name the next day. Of course, it's not always fun and games, so *Brief Encounters* helps you work out if you're able to cope with no-strings sex and gives the best ways to stay safe if you do indulge.

Incredibly useful and lots of fun, *Brief Encounters* is the essential guide to having the ride(s) of your life.

'Feisty, funny and spot on!'
Dr Pam Spurr, author of *The Dating Survival Guide*

'Fascinating, informative, amusing and scary as hell. This book is full of advice aimed at giving women an unfair advantage.'
Mill Millington, author of *Things my Girlfriend and I have Argued About*

Non-fiction: Sex/Relationships
1-904132-66-9
£10.99
$17.95
www.fusionpress.co.uk

I'd Rather be Single than Settle
Satisfied Solitude and How to Achieve It
Emily Dubberley

From our childhood we're fed stories of finding our Prince Charming and living happily ever after with 'The One'. But is being attached really all it's cracked up to be and do we need an 'other half' to be complete?

In *I'd Rather be Single than Settle*, Emily Dubberley upturns the media stereotypes of desperate singletons and blissful couples and explores the *real* world of the single woman. Celebrating the best things about independence – the close friendships and great nights out, the chance to further your career and follow your dreams – she also gives practical advice on overcoming the downsides. Find out how to deal with smug couples and meddlesome mothers who can't accept your solo status, as well as how to beat the blues when the loneliness kicks in.

Packed with case studies from other spirited singles, *I'd Rather be Single than Settle* is the essential guide to singledom. After all, life's too short to settle!

'Singles will be sad no more once they've read this book.'
Tracey Cox, author of *Supersex*

Non-fiction: Self-help/Relationships
1-904132-98-7
UK: £10.99
US: $17.95
www.fusionpress.co.uk

You Must Be My Best Friend...Because I Hate You!
Friendship and How to Survive It
Emily Dubberley

Like love, friendship is an important part of life, but being a good friend isn't always easy. Friends can gossip, hurt your feelings, let you down and, sometimes, they can just be plain dull. But no one admits this or tells you how to deal with it.

Problems can range from jealousy to 'third wheel syndrome', where you introduce two of your closest friends and they hate each other on sight – or seem to like each other more than they like you. Things get more difficult the closer you get. You might face the joys of holidaying together or living together – not to mention complications like dealing with your friend's partner. And then there are the friends that you outgrow.

In *You Must Be My Best Friend ... Because I Hate You!*, Emily Dubberley busts the myth that friendship is all giggling over cocktails. With the help of true-life stories, she surveys every kind of 'bad friend' act and offers consolation, a wry laugh and practical solutions.

Self-help/Relationships
1-904132-76-6
£10.99
$17.95
www.fusionpress.co.uk